Print ISBN: 978-93-5812-829-1

Edition: eBook

Author: Nilesh Bodhi

Publisher: Self Publisher

First Publication Date: 16-Sep-2023

Contact Email contactus@coachfin.in

Contents

Welcoming Failure 4

1.Lack of Clear Goals 7

2.Procrastination 12

3.Lack of Motivation 17

4.Distractions 22

5.Lack of Self Esteem 26

6.Lack of Support 31

7.Unrealistic Expectations 35

8.Not Taking Action 40

9.Lack of Self-Awareness 44

10.Negative Mindset 48

11.Lack of Focus 52

12.Lack of Discipline 56

13.Lack of Consistency 61

14.Lack of Perseverance 65

15.Lack of Patience 70

16.Lack of Time Management 75

17.Lack of Financial Management 79

18.Lack of Communication 83

19.Lack of Networking 88

20.Lack of Leadership 93

21.Lack of Creativity 97

22.Lack of Adaptability 102

23.Lack of Innovation 105

24.Lack of Strategic Thinking 109

25.Lack of Technology Skills 113
26.Lack of Emotional Intelligence 116
27.Lack of Resilience 121
28.Lack of Stress Management 125
29.Lack of Conflict Management 131
30.Lack of Assertiveness 135
31.Lack of Inspiration 139
32.Lack of Initiative 143
33.Lack of Goal Setting 147
34.Lack of Decision Making 151
35.Lack of Risk Taking 155
36.Lack of Trust 159
37.Lack of Integrity 163
38.Lack of Community Involvement 167
39.Fear of Failure 171

PREFACE

Failure is something that everyone experiences at some point in their lives because it is a part of life. However, it's how we handle it and what we take away from it that makes us who we are, not the failure. In this book, we'll be discussing 39 reasons why people fail in life, and the steps that can be taken to overcome them. These reasons include lack of clear goals, procrastination, lack of motivation, distractions, lack of Self Esteem, lack of support, unrealistic expectations, not taking action, lack of self-awareness, Negative mindset, lack of focus, lack of discipline, lack of consistency, lack of perseverance, lack of patience, lack of time management, lack of financial management, lack of communication skills, lack of networking skills, lack of leadership skills, lack of creativity, lack of adaptability, lack of innovation, lack of strategic thinking, lack of technology skills, lack of emotional intelligence, lack of resilience, lack of stress management, lack of conflict management, lack of assertiveness, lack of inspiration, lack of initiative, lack of creativity, lack of decision making skills, lack of risk taking, lack of trust, lack of integrity, lack of community involvement and lack of failure.

It is important to address these reasons to achieve success in life. By recognizing and addressing these potential roadblocks, individuals can take steps to overcome them and pave the way for success. This can include setting clear goals, developing a plan, building a support system, developing self-discipline, time management and organization, self-awareness, self-compassion, and patience, and seeking inspiration and guidance from role models.

It is also important to remember that achieving success is not a one-time event, but rather a continuous process that requires ongoing effort and self-reflection. By being aware of these reasons, we can avoid them and work towards our goals and lead a successful life. We will explore all the causes of failure and how to address them. Whether you're currently struggling with failure or looking to prevent it in the future, this book will provide valuable insights and actionable steps for achieving success in life.

Welcoming Failure

Many times, people think that failing is a horrible thing that should be avoided at all costs. But failure can also offer a chance for development and a priceless lesson. By accepting failure and drawing lessons from our mistakes, we can turn setbacks into opportunities and achieve greater success in life.

One of the key benefits of failing is that it helps us develop our sense of resilience. When we fail, we are forced to own our flaws and limitations. Despite the fact that it could be challenging, this experience gives us the chance to learn from our errors and develop new skills. By accepting failure and using it as a learning experience, we may increase our resilience and enhance our ability to deal with challenges in the future.

Additionally, failure has the capacity to spur originality and creativity. When we face barriers, we are forced to use originality and creativity to solve our problems. This could lead to discoveries and innovations that we otherwise might not have made. By accepting failure and using it as an opportunity to think creatively, we can open new doors and achieve greater success in life.

Finally, failure can foster humility and empathy in us. Failures act as a wake-up call to the fact that none of us are invincible and that we each have our own weaknesses and limitations. This can aid us in developing a stronger empathy for others who are suffering as well as helping us become humbler and more grounded in our own lives. By accepting failure and using it as an opportunity to develop our empathy and humility, we may become better people and achieve more success in all areas of our lives.

The discussion of failures can include the following additions:

1. Failure can help us create a growth mindset. When we experience setbacks, we have a choice. We can either give up or we may seize the opportunity to develop and gain

knowledge from the experience. By choosing to adopt a growth mindset and viewing failure as a steppingstone to achievement, we may enhance our resilience and increase our ability to handle challenges in the future.

2. By failing, we can strengthen our character. When we face obstacles, we are compelled to evaluate our ideals and beliefs. Although this process could be difficult, it can also help us become more self-aware and find our purpose in life. Accepting failure and using it as an opportunity to explore our principles and beliefs might help us become more grounded and sincere as individuals.
3. We may form stronger relationships with one another if we fail. When we fail, we frequently seek help and support from others. This can help us create better bonds with our friends, family, and coworkers. By accepting failure and using it to connect with others, we may expand our network of support and achieve better success in all aspects of our lives.
4. Failure can help us acquire a sense of humor. It is normal to overestimate yourself in the face of disappointment. If we embrace failure and learn to laugh at ourselves, we may develop a sense of humor that will help us navigate life's challenges with greater ease and grace.
5. Failure can help us acquire a sense of gratitude. When faced with adversity, we are reminded of the things we take for granted. This can assist us in developing a greater appreciation for the people and things in our lives that bring us joy and contentment. Accepting failure and using it to create appreciation can help us become happier and more fulfilled individuals.

In conclusion, failure is not something to be worried about or avoided, but something to be embraced. By learning from our mistakes and seeing failure as an opportunity for growth, we can become more resilient, imaginative, and compassionate individuals. The next time you experience a setback, remember that failure is not the end, but rather the beginning of a brand-new window of opportunity for growth and success.

1.Lack of Clear Goals

The inability to achieve one's goals can have a substantial influence on one's capacity to succeed in life. When a person lacks distinct and defined objectives, he or she lacks direction and purpose, making it difficult to discern what they want to achieve and how to attain it. This might leave them feeling unmotivated, uninspired, and unable to put in the required effort to succeed. When faced with hurdles or barriers, it is easy to become diverted, postpone, or just give up if one does not have clear goals. People may also struggle to appropriately prioritize their time and resources, resulting in a lack of productivity and growth. Furthermore, a lack of defined goals can lead to people feeling confused, worried, and overwhelmed since they are unable to focus their attention on the most critical activities. To summarize, it is critical for individuals to set clear and attainable objectives since this provides them with a sense of direction and a road map for success. Individuals who have well-defined objectives are better able to stay focused, motivated, and productive, and they are more likely to overcome the problems and hurdles that they experience along the road.

A lack of defined goals can emerge in several aspects of life, causing people to fail. Here are a couple such examples:

a) Career: If a person does not have defined career objectives, they may struggle to advance in their employment or change occupations frequently, never finding fulfilment or success.
b) Finances: Without defined financial goals, it might be difficult to save money, pay bills on time, or manage debt. This might cause financial stress and make it harder to achieve financial stability.
c) Relationships: A lack of defined relationship objectives can lead to a person attracting unhealthy or unfulfilling relationships or unable to maintain a long-term committed relationship.

d) Health and Wellness: A person may struggle to maintain a healthy lifestyle and attain physical and emotional well-being if they do not have clear health and wellness objectives.
e) Personal Development: A lack of defined personal development objectives can lead to a person feeling trapped, dissatisfied, and unsure of where they are going, causing them to lose out on opportunities for progress and self-discovery.

A lack of defined goals in any of these areas can lead to a sense of aimlessness, dissatisfaction, and, eventually, failure. A person may generate purpose and direction in their life by having clear objectives and working towards them, leading to success and fulfilment.

Once upon a time, there was a guy named Raj who lived in a little village. Raj was well-known for his laziness and lack of enthusiasm in life. He would spend his days lying around with no apparent purpose. His friends and relatives frequently asked him what he wanted to accomplish with his life, but he could never give them an honest response. Raj's wise grandfather sat him down one day and asked him why he never established objectives for himself. Raj said that he had never considered it. His grandfather then told him a story about a bird that never had a purpose in mind and simply went wherever the wind brought it. The bird led an aimless existence and never found happiness. The bird that chose a purpose for itself, flew in a definite route, arrived at its objective, and lived a happy life, on the other hand. Raj finally recognized the value of having specific goals for himself. He made the decision to set a goal of being a successful businessman. He began by setting daily, weekly, and monthly goals, finally reaching his aim. He went on to become a successful businessman, and everyone in the hamlet looked up to him as an example. This narrative demonstrates how a lack of defined goals may lead to aimlessness and a life devoid of meaning. Setting defined objectives, on the other hand, can help one discover direction and lead a successful life.

Specific, Measurable, Achievable, Relevant, and Time-Bound is the acronym for SMART. It is a way to set goals that can help people and organizations get the results they want. We should always aim to set SMART goals because SMART goals are Specific, Measurable, Achievable, Relevant, and Time-bound, making them a useful tool for personal and professional development. Setting SMART targets can help people increase their chances of success and establish a plan for their future.

a. Specific: Individuals may focus on a particular activity or goal because SMART objectives are brief and well-defined.
b. Measurable: SMART targets are quantifiable, allowing you to measure your progress and determine when you've reached your goal.
c. Achievable: SMART goals are realistic and practical since they take into consideration a person's resources and abilities.
d. Relevant: SMART objectives are congruent with a person's values and priorities, ensuring that their efforts are focused on what is most important to them.
e. Time Bound: A deadline for SMART targets promotes a feeling of urgency and accountability.

Individuals may boost their motivation, keep focused on their work, and adjust their plan as needed by utilizing SMART goals. Overall, it provides structure and direction in life, leading to greater accomplishment and fulfilment. This framework can help you focus your efforts, measure your progress, and increase your chances of success. Individuals who create SMART goals are likely to boost their motivation, stay on track, and avoid distractions that may arise when goals are vague or unreachable. With this, tasks are prioritized, resources are allocated, the impact of efforts is evaluated, all of which can lead to the likelihood of success in personal and professional life.
A great illustration of how SMART goals can be applied in the business world is the story of Sarah, a young marketing professional who has just started her career at a large multinational corporation. Sarah was extremely ambitious and eager to succeed, but she quickly realized that her lack of clear goals was preventing her from moving forward. She was frequently working on projects that weren't in line

with her career goals, so she wasn't making much progress toward her long-term career goals. Sarah decided to use the SMART goal-setting method to help her focus on and accomplish her objectives. She started by stating her goals in terms that were precise, measurable, realizable, pertinent, and time bound. Instead of just wanting to be a successful marketer, she set a specific goal, such as "Becoming a Vice President of Marketing at a multinational company within the next ten years."

To achieve this goal, Sarah divided it into smaller, more manageable steps. She set smaller, easier-to-achieve objectives for herself, such as earning a certification in marketing, attending a certain number of industry events annually, and establishing solid relationships with key stakeholders in the marketing industry. She also came up with a way to monitor her progress and set a timetable for each goal. Sarah's plan paid off. By focusing her efforts and keeping track of her progress, she was able to maintain her motivation and make steady progress towards her long-term goal. She was given praise for her efforts and promoted, and before she knew it, she was on her way to becoming a Vice President of Marketing.

This story demonstrates how setting SMART goals can help us focus our efforts and achieve success in both our personal and professional lives. By setting clear, attainable goals, we can stay motivated, overcome challenges, and ultimately achieve our goals.

Below are some ideas for setting focused and realistic goals:

a. Be Specific: Please be as descriptive as possible. Be as detailed as possible when explaining your goal. Rather than creating a broad target like "I want to be fit", make a concrete objective like "I want to lose 10 pounds in the next 6 months".
b. Make it measurable: Make sure your goal is quantifiable so you can track your progress.
c. Set a deadline for yourself: Setting a deadline helps you focus and prioritize your work.

d. Write your goals: Writing them down makes them more tangible and aids in your commitment to them.
e. Break it down: Breaking your goal down into smaller, more manageable phases can assist you in achieving it.
f. Prioritize: Prioritize your goals and concentrate on what is most essential to you.
g. Be realistic: Set objectives that are both attainable and within your ability, while also pushing yourself.
h. Stay motivated: Surround yourself with good influences and look for ways to keep yourself motivated towards your objective.
i. Celebrate tiny victories: To keep yourself motivated, celebrate your success along the road, no matter how minor.
j. Examine and revise: Review your progress on a regular basis and change your objectives as needed to ensure you are on course to meet them.

2.Procrastination

Procrastination is the act of delaying or postponing activities or tasks, frequently without good reason. It's a bad habit that can make it hard to do your job and get where you want to go. There are many reasons why people put things off, including:

a. Reluctance to failure: Some people may put off starting a task out of worry that they won't do it well enough or will make mistakes.
b. Perfectionism: When people set lofty goals for themselves, they may feel overwhelmed by the idea that they won't be able to accomplish them, which causes them to put things off.
c. Boredom or obsession: If a task isn't seen as enjoyable or important, starting it can be difficult.
d. Overwhelm: When faced with a large or complex task, some people may feel overwhelmed and unsure of where to begin, which can lead to procrastination.
e. Distractions: With so many options for distraction, it's easy to put off a task in favor of something more appealing or interesting.
f. Lack of motivation: When a person is not enthusiastic about or motivated by a task, it can be challenging for them to begin it.
g. Negative self-talk: Negative self-talk, such as "I'm not good enough" or "I can never do this," can lead to procrastination.
h. Self-doubt: People who are unsure of their abilities may put off undertakings because they fear that they will never be able to complete them.

Higher levels of stress, lower levels of productivity, and lower levels of
work quality are all negative effects of procrastination. Recognizing and overcoming procrastination is essential to success in life and

achieving one's goals. Addressing the underlying reasons of procrastination and developing healthy habits and strategies can result in increased productivity and success.

Numerous aspects of life can be affected by procrastination, including:

a. Work: Procrastination can lead to project delays, missed deadlines, and lower productivity.
b. Education: Students can put off writing papers or studying for exams, which can lead to lower grades and difficulty graduating on time.
c. Health: It can hurt a person's well-being and increase their likelihood of contracting a disease if they wait to see a doctor, exercise, or eat well.
d. Finances: Procrastinate putting off paying bills, making a budget, or saving for the future can cause financial problems.
e. Relationships: Procrastination can result in missed opportunities to connect with loved ones, which can have a long-term impact on relationships.
f. Personal Growth: A lack of personal development and fulfillment can result from people delaying developing new hobbies, learning new skills, or pursuing personal objectives.
g. House Life: A cluttered and disorganized living space can result from people delaying home improvement projects, organizing, or cleaning.

Procrastination can negatively affect satisfaction, achievement, stress, and frustration in each of these areas. Recognizing when procrastination affects various aspects of life and taking action to overcome it is crucial.

Consider Sarah, a student whose research paper has a week's deadline. However, Sarah spends her time watching television, surfing the internet, and hanging out with friends rather than beginning work on paper. Sarah's anxiety and stress about the paper increase as the deadline approaches, but she still has trouble getting herself to start writing. She eventually realizes that there are only a few hours left until the deadline, so she spends the entire night writing the paper, which results in less quality work and less sleep. This scenario exemplifies the negative effects that procrastination can have on a person's life. Sarah's inability to begin the paper on time resulted in increased stress, subpar work, and a lack of sleep, all of which could have harmed her health and well-being. Sarah could have completed the paper in a more manageable and less stressful manner had she recognized and overcome her procrastination tendencies.

Let us take another example of a professional named John who has had trouble meeting work deadlines. He works long hours and experiences stress and overwhelm due to delaying project completion. John struggles to begin tasks, despite his best efforts, and he frequently finds himself getting sidetracked by email or social media.

John's procrastination likely stems from several factors, including a lack of motivation and a fear of failure. John might put it off until the very last minute when he feels pressured to finish because he is afraid, he won't be able to complete the task up to his high standards. Additionally, John may not find the projects he is working on particularly interesting or fulfilling, making it difficult to begin and contributing to his lack of motivation. John may need to address the underlying causes of his procrastination to overcome his propensity to put things off. This could entail setting goals that are easier to achieve, breaking down tasks into smaller, more manageable steps, and figuring out how to get him more excited about the things he needs to do. John may also benefit from seeking assistance from a coach or counselor to identify and overcome his fears and negative self-perceptions. In conclusion, this illustration emphasizes the significance of identifying and addressing the underlying causes of procrastination to overcome it and lead a life that is both more productive and more satisfying.

Here are some effective strategies for avoiding procrastination:

a. Establish precise goals: Define your goals and subdivide them into smaller, more manageable tasks as the first step. If you know exactly what you want to accomplish and how you will get there, starting can be easier.
b. Put your work first: Make a to-do list and give each item a priority according to how important and urgent it is. Focus on completing the most important tasks first and don't be afraid to delegate or say no to less important ones.
c. Use a timer: By setting a timer for a predetermined amount of time, you can concentrate on completing one task at a time. You can use this to begin and continue.
d. Eliminate all distractions: Find and eliminate sources of distraction such as notifications, social media, and email. Create a distraction-free environment to help you stay motivated and focused.
e. Spend time with yourself: Take care of your mental and physical well-being at the same time. Examples of this include exercising regularly, eating well, getting enough sleep, and planning time for activities you enjoy.
f. Be accountable to yourself: Consider working with a coach or accountability partner to help you stay on track and overcome procrastination.
g. Recognize who you are: Install a system that rewards you with points for completing tasks to keep you motivated. This could be as simple as giving yourself a break or a small reward after completing a task.
h. Change your negative mental attitude: Recognize and reframe negative thoughts like "I can't do this" and "I'm not good enough." Instead, pay attention to how you talk to yourself and remember your abilities and strengths.
i. By implementing these strategies, you can overcome procrastination and achieve your objectives more effectively

and efficiently. If you want to get rid of procrastination, you need to be patient and keep trying because changing habits can take time and practice.

Finally, Procrastination is a problem that many people must deal with on a regular basis. It can cause problems in our lives, like more stress and less good work. However, it is a behavior that can be overcome with the right strategies and mindset.

To overcome procrastination, effective strategies include prioritizing tasks, setting clear goals, removing distractions, practicing self-care, and seeking accountability. Motivating and sustaining progress can also be helped by reframing negative thoughts and establishing a reward system.

In conclusion, procrastination is a problem that can be resolved through hard work and time management. By using effective strategies and maintaining a positive outlook, we can accomplish our goals and lead lives that are more fulfilling and productive.

3.Lack of Motivation

Lack of motivation is defined as a lack of interest in activities or tasks, a sense of disinterest to work toward a goal. It can show up as a lack of enthusiasm, interest, and energy, making it hard to start and keep working on projects or tasks or to feel motivated to do so. People who lack motivation may have trouble starting and finishing projects, losing interest in activities they used to enjoy, or being motivated to change their lives. A lack of motivation can have a short-term or long-term effect on work, relationships, personal growth, and physical and mental health. In some cases, it may be connected to a specific circumstance, such as a change in circumstances or a particular obstacle, while in other cases, it may be a more widespread and persistent problem. Regardless of the cause, a lack of motivation can have a negative impact on one's well-being and quality of life. It can cause feelings of boredom, frustration, and low self-esteem as well as prevent people from realizing their full potential. By recognizing the underlying causes of low motivation and taking action to address them, individuals can overcome this obstacle and lead lives that are both more fulfilling and productive.

People who lack motivation may find it difficult to begin and complete projects, lose interest in activities they used to enjoy, or find it difficult to motivate themselves to make changes in their lives. Work, relationships, personal development, physical and mental health can all be affected by a lack of motivation, which can be a short-term or long-term problem. It may be related to a specific circumstance, such as a change in circumstances or a particular obstacle, in some instances, while in other instances, it may be a more pervasive and persistent issue. Lack of motivation can have a negative impact on one's well-being and quality of life, regardless of the cause. It can prevent people from realizing their full potential and cause feelings of boredom, frustration, and low self-esteem. People can overcome this obstacle and lead lives that are more satisfying and productive by becoming aware of the root causes of low motivation and taking action to address them.

Lack of motivation can be caused by several things, including:

a. Problems with physical health: An illness, chronic fatigue, or pain can sap motivation and make it hard to do things.
b. Issues with mental health: By hindering one's ability to concentrate and maintain a positive outlook, depression, anxiety, stress, and burnout can affect motivation.
c. Boredom or lack of fulfillment: Boredom and a lack of motivation can result from doing the same things over and over or feeling stuck in a job or situation that doesn't give you much satisfaction.
d. Low self-esteem: It can be difficult to believe in one's own abilities and goals when one feels inadequate or unworthy, which can result in low motivation.
e. Unmet needs or wants: A lack of motivation can result from feeling unfulfilled in one's personal or professional life.
f. Negative self-talk or beliefs: Thinking things like "I'm not good enough" or "I can't do this" can make you less motivated and make you avoid challenges or activities.
g. Lack of structure or direction: It can be hard to stay focused and motivated when there isn't a clear plan or goal.
h. Factors in the environment: Motivation and well-being can be affected by living in a stressful, uninspiring, or cluttered environment.
i. Monetary stress: Problems with money can cause stress and anxiety, which can make it hard to get things done.
j. Strained relationships: Conflicts or problems in personal or professional relationships can make people less motivated by making them feel stressed out and lowering their self-esteem.

Although the specific reasons for a person's lack of motivation can vary, these are some of the most common causes. People can develop strategies to overcome low motivation and enhance their quality of life with the assistance of an understanding of the underlying causes.

Here are some ways to avoid feeling unmotivated:

a. Give self-care priority: Taking care of one's physical and mental health by exercising, eating well, and getting enough sleep can increase one's motivation and energy levels.
b. Set attainable objectives: To assist in gaining momentum and a sense of accomplishment, break larger objectives down into smaller, more manageable tasks.
c. Find meaning and purpose: Engaging in activities or responsibilities that are in line with one's personal values and interests can boost one's motivation and level of contentment.
d. Establish relationships: Motivation and a sense of belonging can be helped by social support from friends, family, or a support group.
e. You should surround yourself with positive people: Building self-confidence and motivation can be helped by surrounding oneself with positive, supportive people.
f. Change your surroundings: A more energizing and inspiring atmosphere can be created by making changes to your physical environment, such as getting rid of clutter or decorating with plants or other decorations.
g. Try something new: Experimenting with new hobbies and activities can help you find new interests and motivations and combat boredom.
h. Make gratitude a habit: By fostering a more upbeat outlook, focusing on one's strengths rather than one's weaknesses can help motivate one to achieve their goals.
i. Prioritize progress over perfection: Instead of striving for perfection, focus on progress toward goals and small victories to maintain motivation and a sense of accomplishment.
j. Get expert assistance: Seeking assistance from a mental health professional can be beneficial if a mental health issue, such as depression or anxiety, is underlying the lack of motivation.

Keep in mind that finding the strategies that work best for each person may take time and vary from person to person. However, people can overcome their lack of motivation and achieve their goals by making changes and acting.

Lara was employed as a sales representative for the past five years. She used to enjoy her job, but in recent months she has felt unmotivated and unsatisfied. Sarah has noticed that she consistently puts things off and lacks motivation and energy when it comes to completing tasks. Lara thinks back and realizes that her lack of motivation is caused by the fact that she feels stuck in her job because she hasn't had any opportunities to grow or develop. Additionally, she has felt undervalued and underappreciated by her supervisor and coworkers. She is losing motivation because of the negative and uninspiring work environment that has resulted from the combination of these elements. Lara decides to act in order to overcome her lack of motivation. In addition to beginning her search for new employment opportunities that are in line with her values and interests, she establishes attainable objectives for herself, such as identifying new challenges and opportunities within her current position. Sarah also starts to put herself first, making time for her favorite hobbies and exercise. In addition, she seeks assistance from family and friends and joins a professional organization to network with other professionals in her field. Lara can regain her motivation and begin making positive changes to her life by taking these steps. She eventually gets a new job that gives her the growth and fulfillment she has been looking for, and she becomes more focused and energized. This illustration exemplifies how taking a proactive stance and adjusting can assist individuals in overcoming a lack of motivation and achieving their objectives.

In conclusion, many people experience a lack of motivation at various points in their lives, which is a widespread issue. Potential causes include boredom, unfulfilling personal or professional circumstances, and mental health issues.

Nevertheless, it is essential to acknowledge that a lack of motivation is not permanent and can be overcome through the use of the appropriate strategies and actions. Setting attainable goals, participating in activities that align with their personal values and interests, seeking support from others, and prioritizing self-care are all ways that individuals can increase their motivation and achieve their objectives.

It can take time and effort to overcome lack of motivation, so it is important to be understanding and patient with oneself. However, individuals who take a proactive approach and persevere can achieve their goals and make positive changes to their lives.

4.Distractions

Distractions are anything that keeps a person from concentrating on the task at hand and makes it hard for them to be productive. There are numerous types of distractions, including external, internal, technological, environmental, social, and mental distractions. Outside distractions, such as noise, visual stimulation, or interruptions from other individuals. Distractions from inside, such as thoughts, feelings, or urges. Technology-related distractions, such as phone or computer notifications. Distractions from the environment, such as an uncomfortable workplace or poor lighting. Social distractions, such as conversing with coworkers or friends during work hours. Mental distractions include worries, stress, and boredom.

There are many kinds of distractions, some of which include:

a. Technology: Due to the prevalence of technology, such as email, instant messaging, and social media, people are exposed to an ever-increasing number of distractions.
b. Environment: Inadequate lighting, a noisy or cluttered workspace, and other aspects of the environment can also cause distractions.
c. Personal factors: Personal factors like boredom, anxiety, and stress can also cause distractions.
d. Lack of focus: Disciplined and unfocused individuals may occasionally become easily distracted. They might have trouble keeping their attention on the task at hand or they might be easily distracted by thoughts or activities that have nothing to do with the task at hand.
e. Poor with time management: As a result of feeling rushed or overwhelmed, people who struggle to effectively manage their time are also more likely to become sidetracked.

f. Not enough sleep: Insufficient sleep can also cause distractions because fatigue and sleepiness can make it difficult to concentrate and work productively.
g. Substance: Substance abuse can also lead to distractions because alcohol and drugs can make it harder to focus and make judgments.

By identifying and addressing the factors that lead to distractions, individuals can take steps to reduce them, improve their focus, and increase their productivity.

Some methods that can help people focus better and avoid being distracted are as follows:

a. Limit the use of technology: Set aside specific times for checking emails and social media, turn off notifications, and put away electronic devices when working or studying.
b. Make environment conducive: To reduce distractions, create a workspace that is clutter-free, well-lit, and comfortable.
c. Practicing mindfulness as habit: By bringing awareness to the present moment and reducing stress and anxiety, mindfulness can assist individuals in remaining focused and minimizing the number of distractions.
d. Set attainable goals: Setting attainable goals can help people stay focused on what's important and avoid getting distracted by things that don't matter.
e. Make sleep a priority: It is essential to get enough sleep to avoid fatigue and improve focus.
f. Develop self-control: Because it requires individuals to make conscious decisions about what they allow to distract them and what they ignore, self-discipline is essential for avoiding distractions.
g. Taking breaks: Breaks on a regular basis can help you focus better and avoid burnout.

h. Learn how to manage your time: Strategies for effective time management can help people stay focused and organized, lowering the likelihood of being distracted.
i. Seek assistance: Individuals can address personal factors that contribute to distractions by speaking with friends, family, or a mental health professional.

People can improve their productivity and overall well-being by implementing these strategies, which can also help them focus better and reduce their number of distractions.

A Tel Aviv-based software engineer is working on a crucial client project. However, his work is constantly disrupted by notifications from social media, text messages, and emails on his phone. Additionally, there is a lot of noise in the open-plan office, with coworkers talking and phones ringing. In addition, the engineer is distracted by the stress of a forthcoming deadline. The software engineer employs a few strategies to reduce distractions and improve his concentration. He puts his phone in a different room and disables notifications on it. Additionally, to reduce office noise, he wears headphones with noise-cancellation features. He takes breaks every hour to stretch and walk around and sets daily goals that are doable. He also uses deep breathing and mindfulness to reduce stress and anxiety. The software engineer is able to focus better and finish the project on time, to the client's delight, by employing these tactics.

A London-based college student is studying for her exams. She is, however, easily distracted by the internet and her phone. She finds herself either distracted by online videos or checking her social media accounts when she tries to study. She also finds it difficult to concentrate because her roommates are noisy. The college student employs a few strategies to improve her concentration and avoid being distracted. She moves her phone to a different room and disables notifications on her phone. She also restricts her access to distracting websites while she is studying by using a website blocker. She breaks for stretching and walking around every hour and sets attainable goals for the study sessions. She also uses deep breathing and mindfulness to reduce stress and anxiety. The college student is able to improve her focus and score well on her exams by implementing these strategies.

Because distractions can prevent people from achieving their objectives and reduce focus and engagement, distractions can have a significant impact on an individual's productivity and well-being. Technology, noise, personal stress, and unimportant tasks are just a few distractions. People can use a variety of strategies, including limiting their use of technology, creating a conducive environment, practicing mindfulness, setting achievable goals, taking breaks, practicing self-discipline, time management, and seeking support, to avoid being distracted. Individuals can improve their focus, productivity, and well-being as a whole by minimizing distractions.

5.Lack of Self Esteem

Lack of confidence in one's abilities and value as a person is known as low self-esteem. People who have low self-esteem frequently have negative thoughts and beliefs about themselves. They may also frequently experience feelings of self-doubt or believe that they are not good enough. This can influence their relationships, careers, and happiness. It can also create a vicious cycle in which negative thoughts and actions reinforce one another. Childhood experiences, abuse, or neglect, bullying, and cultural or societal messages that emphasize certain standards of beauty, success, and worth can all contribute to low self-esteem. However, it is also possible to improve one's self-esteem through therapy, positive lifestyle changes, and self-reflection.

A person's low self-esteem can manifest in a variety of ways and have an impact on a variety of life areas. Among the most typical symptoms are:

a. Negative self-talk and criticism of oneself: People who have low self-esteem may frequently engage in harsh and negative inner dialogue, frequently praising both themselves and their abilities.
b. Inability to accept praise: Because they believe they are not worthy of praise, people who have low self-esteem may find it difficult to accept compliments and constructive criticism.
c. Aversion to failure: People who have low self-esteem may be afraid of failing, which prevents them from trying new things or taking risks.
d. Inability to establish boundaries: Because they are afraid of being rejected or disapproved of people with low self-esteem may find it difficult to say "no" to other people or establish healthy boundaries.
e. Inability to establish and maintain relationships: Because people with low self-esteem may doubt their own worth and

believe they are unworthy of love and affection; it can be difficult for them to establish and maintain healthy relationships.

f. Continually seeking others' approval: People who have low self-esteem may constantly seek approval and assurance for their actions and decisions from others.

A significant impediment to personal development and happiness can be low self-esteem. However, it is possible to work on improving self-esteem and developing a healthier sense of self with the assistance of friends, family, and mental health professionals.

There are numerous potential causes of low self-esteem, some of which include:

a. Memories from adolescence: A person's self-esteem and beliefs about themselves can be impacted by negative childhood experiences like abuse, neglect, or criticism from parents or other caregivers.
b. Emotional trauma: Self-esteem can also be affected in the long run by traumatic events like physical or emotional abuse, sexual assault, or the death of a loved one.
c. Cultural and social factors: A person's sense of self-worth can be influenced by messages about what it means to be beautiful, successful, and valuable in society and culture.
d. Comparisons to other people: Low self-esteem can be exacerbated by comparing oneself to others, particularly through social media, which can elicit feelings of inadequacy and insecurity.
e. Conditions related to the mind: Low self-esteem can be exacerbated by mental health conditions like anxiety and depression, which can cause negative thoughts and feelings to become recurrent and cause problems in daily life.

f. Drug addiction: Substance abuse and addiction can influence self-esteem since substance use can generate emotions of shame and worthlessness.

It is essential to keep in mind that every individual experience fluctuation in their self-esteem and that these factors can interact with one another to influence an individual's overall sense of self-worth. However, it is possible to work on improving one's sense of self-worth and self-esteem with the help of resources and support.

Improved self-esteem and avoiding life's distractions can be achieved using the following methods:

a. Show yourself compassion: Instead of being overly critical or harsh, treat yourself with kindness and understanding. Talk to yourself as you would to a friend, focusing on your accomplishments and strengths.
b. Repel negative thinking: When negative thoughts occur, actively challenge them with evidence-based, more upbeat viewpoints.
c. Keep your values in mind: Make an effort to live in accordance with your core values by spending time identifying them. This can help you feel more confident in your decisions and give you a sense of purpose.
d. Be surrounded by positive people: Limit your exposure to negativity by surrounding yourself with friends and family who support and encourage you.
e. Set attainable objectives: Celebrate your progress and successes as you work toward your goals, which should be attainable and based on reality. Your self-esteem and confidence may benefit from this.
f. Practice self-care: Eat well, exercise, and engage in activities that make you happy and help you relax are all good for your mental and physical health.

g. Get professional assistance: Consider seeking assistance from a mental health professional if low self-esteem is affecting your daily life. Working through the underlying causes of low self-esteem and developing a more positive self-image can be accomplished through therapy.

It is essential to keep in mind that building self-esteem is a process, and it may take some time before you notice changes that last. However, it is possible to cultivate a more positive self-image and avoid life's distractions with persistence and a commitment to self-improvement.

28-year-old Priya from Mumbai was constantly criticized as a child for the choices she made regarding her education and career. She never succeeded in meeting her parents' expectations, resulting in feelings of inadequacy and low self-esteem. Many aspects of Priya's life have been impacted by her low self-esteem. She is constantly seeking approval and validation from her coworkers and has difficulty asserting herself at work. Due to her fear of being rejected and disappointed, she also finds it difficult to establish and maintain intimate relationships. Priya's negative feelings and thoughts are now a constant distraction that affects her day-to-day life and impedes her personal and professional development. She has, however, decided to seek assistance and work on improving her self-esteem. She has begun seeing a therapist, who is assisting her in challenging her negative beliefs and concentrating on her accomplishments and strengths. Priya is also working hard to take care of herself and spend time with friends and family who are there for her. Low self-esteem can have a negative impact on a person's life in several ways. However, it is essential to keep in mind that every person's experience of low self-esteem is unique and that, with the help of resources and support, self-esteem and self-image can be improved.

A challenging and persistent problem, low self-esteem can have an impact on many aspects of a person's life. It can come from several different things, like traumatic events in childhood, social and cultural factors, comparing oneself to other people, mental health issues, and substance abuse.

However, it is essential to keep in mind that self-esteem is a fluid construct that, with effort and support, can evolve over time. Therapy, self-compassion, positive self-talk, and participating in activities that bring joy and fulfillment are just a few of the many strategies and resources that can be used to boost self-esteem.

It is essential to seek assistance and resources if you or someone you know is experiencing low self-esteem to address the underlying causes and cultivate a more positive self-image. It is possible to cultivate self-esteem and lead a fulfilling life free of distractions with persistence and a commitment to self-improvement.

6.Lack of Support

The absence of assistance, encouragement, or direction from others is referred to as "lack of support." Emotional, social, financial, and practical support are just a few examples. A lack of emotional connection with others, being in an environment where support is not readily available or going through a traumatic event that results in the loss of support from friends, family, or other sources are all potential causes of lack of support. People who lack assistance may feel alienated, overwhelmed, and separated from others. This can have a significant impact on one's mental and emotional well-being, as well as financial troubles and an increased risk of stress and burnout. It is crucial to remember, however, that there are several tools and solutions available to assist people who are feeling a lack of support. Building a support network, getting professional help, engaging in self-care, and reaching out to friends and family may all be examples of this.

It is possible to overcome the problems connected with a lack of support and develop a more rewarding, supportive life with work and a dedication to self-improvement.

There are various reasons for a lack of support, among them are:

a. Geographic distance: Living far away from friends, family, and support networks can make receiving emotional and financial help challenging.
b. Socioeconomic status: Individuals who are struggling financially may have a more difficult time accessing services and support networks.
c. Personal factors: Trauma, mental health issues, and other personal variables might make it difficult for people to connect with others and receive help.
d. Stigma: The stigma associated with some disorders, such as mental health concerns, can discourage people from getting help and engaging with others.

e. Communication challenges: Problems with communication, misunderstandings, and disputes with friends and family can all lead to a lack of support.
f. Changes in life: Life transitions such as divorce, retirement, or the loss of a loved one can disrupt support networks and result in a lack of support.

It's critical to understand that the causes of a lack of support are multifaceted and might differ from person to person. Nonetheless, finding resources and assistance can assist individuals in overcoming the difficulties connected with a lack of support.

To avoid life's distractions, there are some solutions to a lack of support:

a. Establishing a solid support system: Be open, trustworthy, and supportive to build new relationships and maintain existing ones with people who share your values and interests.
b. Joining a support group: Find a group of people who have been through similar difficulties and want to feel like they belong and have a sense of community.
c. Getting professional assistance: Take into consideration seeing a therapist for emotional support, direction, and assistance with coping mechanisms.
d. Giving oneself care: Engage in hobbies, exercise, and other activities that bring joy and help you relax.
e. Getting in touch with family and friends: Be honest about your needs and how they can assist you and don't be afraid to ask for help from friends and family.

Meet Anika, a woman from New Delhi who is 32 years old. Anika is experiencing feelings of loneliness and isolation because of a significant life change, such as a divorce or the death of a loved one. She used to have a group of close friends and family, but they have grown distant and have stopped responding to her needs. Anika lacks direction in her life and is feeling overwhelmed. She is feeling drained and unmotivated at work and is having trouble focusing. She is unable to deal with her feelings of isolation and lack of support, despite her best efforts. As a solution to her lack of support, Anika has decided to seek assistance. She has started going to a support group for people who have gone through the same problems as her and has found solace in connecting with other people who know what she is going through. She is also contacting friends and family, and she has discovered that communicating her requirements openly and honestly has improved her relationships with them.

A single parent who has lost their job because of the COVID-19 pandemic could serve as an actual illustration of the lack of financial support. Without a consistent source of income, this person may have difficulty meeting their financial obligations and supporting their family. They might have trouble coming up with money to pay for things like food, housing, and medical bills, and they might also be stressed out financially and worried about the future.

To address the lack of financial support, the individual may look for resources in this scenario. This might entail seeking financial assistance from the government or community organizations, consulting a financial advisor, or investigating different ways to earn money, like freelancing or starting a small business.

Recognizing that having access to resources and support is a crucial step in overcoming obstacles brought on by a lack of financial support is essential to achieving well-being. It is possible to construct a financial future that is more stable and secure with effort and a commitment to self-improvement.

In conclusion, experiencing a lack of support can be difficult and overwhelming, but there are resources and strategies available to assist in coping with the accompanying feelings of loneliness and isolation. Overcoming feelings of a lack of support and avoiding life's distractions can all be accomplished by engaging in self-care, establishing a strong support network, and seeking professional assistance.

Lack of emotional and financial support refers to the absence of emotional and financial assistance, encouragement, and guidance from others. Lack of emotional support can involve feelings of loneliness, isolation, and a sense of disconnection from others. It can be caused by factors such as a lack of meaningful relationships, a traumatic event that leads to the loss of support or living in an environment where emotional support is not readily available. Lack of financial support can involve difficulties making ends meet, paying bills, and achieving financial stability. It can be caused by factors such as job loss, underemployment, or living in an environment with limited financial resources. It is important to seek support and resources to address the challenges of lack of emotional and financial support. With effort and a commitment to self-improvement, it is possible to build a strong support network, improve financial stability, and live a fulfilling, distraction-free life.

Individuals and families can suffer severe consequences from a lack of emotional and financial support. One's self-esteem, confidence, and happiness can all be impacted by emotional support, which is critical to mental health. Anxiety, depression, and feelings of loneliness can all result from a lack of emotional support. Like how basic needs can be met and financial stability achieved, financial support is essential. Individuals and families may experience financial stress and insecurity if they are unable to pay for housing, food, and other necessities. This can also have long-term effects, like making it hard to save for retirement or pay for school.

When individuals are confronted with a lack of emotional and financial support, it is essential for them to seek assistance from friends, family, and community resources. Support groups, financial assistance programs, and counseling services are all examples of this. People can work to overcome these obstacles and improve their overall well-being by asking for help.

7.Unrealistic Expectations

Expectations that are unrealistic, unrealistically optimistic, or not grounded in reality are known as unrealistic expectations. They can be established by oneself or by others. When they are not met, unrealistic expectations can result in dissatisfaction, anger, and a sense of failure. A person may, for instance, have unreasonable expectations regarding their performance at a new job, their romantic relationship, or their financial success. The individual may be setting themselves up for disappointment and frustration if these expectations are not in line with the circumstances. It's important to be aware of expectations that aren't realistic and work toward setting goals and expectations that are doable and attainable. Taking a step back, evaluating the situation objectively, and considering one's strengths and weaknesses are all examples of this. Individuals can reduce feelings of disappointment and frustration and increase their chances of success by setting realistic expectations. Expectations that are not based on an outcome that is either achievable or realistic are unrealistic. They can be based on personal beliefs, societal norms, or experiences from the past that don't line up with the current situation. People may experience negative emotions like anger, frustration, and disappointment when these expectations are not met. Examples of unrealistic expectations include the following:

a. Expecting flawless outcomes every time: This kind of expectation frequently stems from the notion that one must always be successful.
b. Expecting success right away: Expecting immediate results despite the effort and time required to achieve a goal is another example of unrealistic expectations.
c. Expecting other people to take care of you: It is unreasonable to expect other people to always meet your practical or emotional needs without taking into account their own emotions or circumstances.
d. Making comparisons with others: Because everyone's life experiences and circumstances are unique, it can be

unrealistic to compare oneself to others and expect similar outcomes.

Unrealistic expectations can have a negative impact on relationships, work, and overall well-being as well as cause disappointment and frustration. Realistic expectations must be recognized and corrected by setting attainable goals and considering the facts of the situation in question to avoid this.

Several things can lead to unrealistic expectations, including:

a. Influences from culture and society: Media, society, and advertising all have the potential to instill unfounded expectations about what constitutes normal or desirable behavior, behavior, relationships, and success.
b. Personal convictions and values: Unrealistic expectations can also be caused by individual values and beliefs, especially when it comes to relationships, careers, and personal goals.
c. Previous experiences: Expectations about the future can be based on past experiences, especially those that were positive. For instance, if a person has had a particularly fruitful experience in a particular field, they might anticipate similar success in all their subsequent endeavors.
d. Cognitive Biases: People may develop overly optimistic views of their own capabilities and the outcomes they can anticipate because of certain cognitive biases, such as the optimism bias.
e. Lack of knowledge: People may also have unrealistic expectations when they lack sufficient knowledge or experience in a particular field. For instance, a person who has never purchased a home may have unreasonable expectations regarding the time, effort, and costs involved.
f. Obligation to conform: It's possible that people will adopt unattainable standards for themselves as a result of feeling

pressured to meet the standards set by others.

When our expectations are not met, they can result in disappointment, frustration, and stress, so it's important to be aware of them and critically examine them.

There are a few methods that can assist you in managing life's unrealistic expectations:

a. Setting attainable objectives: Set goals that are attainable, realistic, and in line with your values after reflecting on what truly matters to you. Be open with yourself about what you can and can't realistically accomplish.
b. Control your expectations: Manage your own expectations and those of others by taking charge. Don't take on more than you can handle; communicate clearly what you can and cannot do.
c. Develop self-awareness: Increase your awareness of your thought patterns and expectations by engaging in self-reflection. This can assist you in determining when you are setting unreasonable expectations for yourself or others and in making any necessary adjustments.
d. Seek assistance: Be surrounded by people who will encourage you and assist you in managing your expectations. For assistance, think about contacting friends, family, or a mental health professional.
e. Make gratitude a habit: Concentrate on the good things in your life and cultivate gratitude. Even when things are not going according to plan, this can assist you in maintaining a more upbeat and realistic outlook.
f. Acknowledge disappointment: It is essential to be able to accept and manage disappointment in a healthy manner because expectations are not always met. Concentrate on what

you can take away from the experience and how you can improve in the future.

g. Limit your exposure to expectations that aren't true: Reduce your exposure to media, advertising, and other sources' unrealistic expectations. Focus on your own values and goals and surround yourself with people who are realistic and supportive.

You can develop more realistic expectations and improve your overall well-being with patience, self-awareness, and support. However, managing unrealistic expectations is a process that may take some time.

A recent college graduate who anticipates landing their dream job immediately after graduation is a real-world illustration of unrealistic expectations. They quickly discover that the job market is highly competitive and that finding the right job takes time, despite having a solid resume and good education. Because they did not fully comprehend the job market, the competition for jobs, or the time and effort required to find the right job, this individual may have had expectations that were too high. Friends, family, or societal expectations that college graduates should be able to find high-paying jobs immediately may also have had an impact. The individual could gain from learning more about the job market and what it takes to find a job that fits their skills and interests, seeking support from mentors or career counselors, and setting realistic goals in this scenario. They might be able to lower their levels of stress and anxiety because of doing this, and their chances of finding a job that is both fulfilling and important might rise as a result.

In conclusion, having life's unmet expectations can significantly affect our mental health and wellbeing. When they aren't met, they can make us feel overwhelmed and worn out as well as cause us to be disappointed, irritated, and stressed. Having realistic expectations, on the other hand, can help us feel more in control of our lives, boost our motivation, and aid in our personal development and happiness. It's essential to strike a balance between having acceptable expectations and carrying on with our personal development. We can strike a healthy balance between having expectations and enjoying the journey toward our goals by adopting a growth mindset. So, it's important to know where our expectations come from and think critically about whether they are based on accurate information or if they are influenced by societal, cultural, or personal biases. We can lessen the negative effects of having unrealistic expectations and improve our well-being if we take the time to set attainable goals, communicate effectively with others, and seek assistance when we need it.

Keep in mind that it is acceptable to have goals and to work toward achieving our goals in life. But it's just as important to be aware of the standards we set for ourselves and others and to understand that growth and success frequently require patience, effort, and time.

8.Not Taking Action

Lack of action or not taking action in life is the inability to carry out one's obligations, desires, or goals. It refers to putting off or delaying taking the steps necessary to advance or succeed in a certain area of life. This might occur in a personal, professional, or other setting. Several factors, including a fear of failure, a lack of motivation, or an absence of clarity or direction, can lead to inaction. It might also be brought on by feeling overburdened or lacking the courage to start. Taking no action can impede people from realizing their potential and result in feelings of dissatisfaction and disappointment, regardless of the motivation. Therefore, it's critical to recognize the causes of inaction and take action to address them. This can entail reaching out for assistance, creating a strategy, establishing realistic goals, and making steady progress in little steps. People can raise their drive, boost their confidence, and accomplish their goals by acting and moving forward.

There are many reasons why people do not act in life, including:

a. Aversion to failure: People who are afraid of failing can avoid acting because they are afraid of failing to achieve their objectives or making mistakes.
b. Lack of drive: If a person believes that their goals are not in line with their values or interests, they may lack the inspiration or motivation to act.
c. Overwhelm: People may feel overwhelmed and unsure of where to begin when faced with complex or challenging tasks, preventing them from acting.
d. Clarity or lack of direction: People may have difficulty achieving their objectives if they are unsure of what they want or how to get there.
e. Perfectionism: People who believe that their actions must be flawless to succeed may avoid taking any action at all.

f. Procrastination: The act of delaying or putting off tasks is known as procrastination, and it can be a major factor in life inaction.
g. Lack of faith: People who lack confidence may avoid action because they are afraid of failing or being criticized by others.
h. Adverse self-talk: Self-doubt and negative self-talk can also prevent people from acting because they may believe they are not worthy of success or capable of it.

Individuals can take steps to overcome the obstacles they face and advance toward their objectives once they are aware of the reasons behind their lack of action. This might entail getting help, planning, making goals that are doable, taking small but consistent steps toward their goals.

Here are some remedies if you don't act in your life:

a. Identify attainable goals and set them: A smart way to start is by breaking down your objective into smaller, more doable tasks. Set reasonable, measurable goals and track your development frequently.
b. Develop a plan: Plan outlining the measures you must take to accomplish your goals, including duties and due dates. You can stay motivated and focused by putting a plan in place.
c. Start off modestly: Start by making achievable, small-step progress that boosts your self-assurance and momentum. These inconsequential behaviors may ultimately produce important results.
d. Practice self-care: Take care of your mental, emotional, and physical health so that you can feel more inspired and motivated to act.
e. Seek help: Surround yourself with upbeat, motivating people who can encourage you and help you stay on course. You

might also look for a coach or mentor who can assist you in maintaining focus and overcoming obstacles.

f. Face your phobias: Face it. The fear of failure or rejection can cause people to delay acting. List your anxieties and devise strategies for overcoming them.
g. Cultivate growth mindset: Adopt a "growth attitude" and understand that progress often requires time, effort, and patience. Adopt a growth attitude and focus on learning and progress rather than trying to be perfect.
h. Be Accountable: Finally, accept accountability for your actions by recognizing that you are in control of your life. Stop coming up with justifications and start taking the necessary steps to achieve your goals.

By putting these answers into practice, people can overcome the challenges of not acting in life and move closer to their goals and aspirations.

A person who has always aspired to establish their own business but has not taken any measures to make it a reality could serve as a real-life example of someone who is not acting in life. They might not act for a variety of reasons, including a fear of failing, a lack of finances, or a lack of faith in their capacity for success. Despite having dreams, this person can spend their days at a job they detest and refrain from taking any steps to launch their own business. They could give reasons why they can't start a firm, including "I don't have enough money to do so" or "I'm not sure whether I have what it takes to be an entrepreneur."

But by being inactive, this person is passing up the chance to follow their dreams and improve both their own and other people's lives. To get past this, they may start by planning, defining specific, attainable goals, and moving slowly in that direction by doing market research, connecting with others in the industry, and conserving money. They can boost their confidence and raise their chances of success by acting and moving forward.

Not acting in life can prevent people from fulfilling their potential and accomplishing their goals. Inaction can result in feelings of unhappiness, regret, and unmet expectations. Individual's risk missing out on chances to learn, develop, and improve both their own and other people's lives by doing nothing.

However, it's crucial to understand that not acting is a frequent problem that may be solved. People can overcome the difficulties of not acting and advance towards their goals by making specific, attainable goals, creating a plan, taking baby actions, and getting support.

In conclusion, acting towards one's goals is essential for both personal and professional development, and people should work to remove any barriers that stand in their way. Individuals can attain their full potential, accomplish their goals, and lead rewarding lives by acting.

9.Lack of Self-Awareness

Lack of self-awareness is characterized by ignorance or lack of perception of one's own thoughts, feelings, and behaviors. Lack of self-awareness can make it difficult for someone to comprehend their own motives, feelings, and beliefs as well as their influence on others. Lack of self-awareness can cause a variety of issues, such as subpar decision-making, inadequate communication, and trouble establishing and keeping good relationships. Additionally, it can exacerbate feelings of uncertainty, worry, and despair. Lack of self-awareness can lead to impulsive behavior in those who don't think things through first. They might also have a hard time identifying their own advantages and disadvantages, which can hinder both their personal and professional development. Self-awareness can be fostered in a variety of ways, such as through self-reflection and mindfulness, getting input from others, and taking part in activities that make one question their assumptions and worldviews. People can strengthen their connections with others, understand themselves better, and make better judgements by developing their self-awareness.

Lack of self-awareness in life can be caused by several things, including:

a. Avoiding introspection: Some people may avoid reflecting on their own thoughts, feelings, and actions internally. They may have difficulty understanding their own motives and feelings because of this.
b. Aversion to criticism: Self-reflection may be avoided by some people because they are afraid of being criticized or learning about their shortcomings.
c. Unconscious biases: Everyone has unconscious biases, which can make it hard to see things clearly and make it hard to be aware of oneself.

d. Abstinence from emotion: A lack of self-awareness can also be caused by suppressing emotions or avoiding confronting difficult feelings.
e. Factors in the environment: A person's level of self-awareness can also be affected by the circumstances in which they were raised. For instance, developing self-awareness may be difficult for those who grow up in environments where their thoughts and feelings are not acknowledged or validated.
f. Issues with mental health: An individual's capacity to be self-aware can be impacted by certain mental health conditions like depression or anxiety.
g. Lack of self-reflection: It can be difficult for people to develop self-awareness if they don't take the time to think about their feelings and experiences.

A lack of self-awareness can have a negative impact on one's life, but it is a challenge that can be overcome with effort and a commitment to personal development. It is important to recognize this.

A lack of self-awareness can be overcome in several ways, including the following:

a. Self-reflection and meditation: Self-awareness can be improved by practicing mindfulness and taking time to observe one's thoughts, emotions, and actions.
b. Get feedback from others: A person's behavior and impact on others can be better understood by asking trusted friends, family, or coworkers for feedback.
c. Take part in activities that challenge assumptions: Self-awareness can be improved by engaging in activities that test one's assumptions and beliefs, like traveling to new places or learning about other cultures.

d. Journaling: Regularly jotting down one's thoughts and feelings can help one become more self-aware and gain a deeper comprehension of one's own motivations and feelings.
e. Seek treatment: A supportive setting for self-exploration and self-awareness can be created through therapy.
f. Show yourself compassion: Instead of being critical of oneself, it can be helpful to become more self-aware and have a better relationship with oneself to treat oneself with kindness and understanding.
g. Try out brand-new experiences: Extending one's comfort zone and trying new things can also help one become more self-aware and gain new perspectives.

People can understand themselves better, make better decisions, and have better relationships with others if they make an intentional effort to become more self-aware.

An actual illustration of a person's lack of self-awareness is when they frequently get into arguments with friends and family. They are unable to comprehend how their actions are causing problems, even though others have repeatedly complained about them. They might, without realizing it, interrupt other people during conversations or be insensitive to the feelings of others. This individual may have developed a pattern of not paying attention to their own emotions and behavior because of growing up in an environment where their thoughts and feelings were not acknowledged. They might also avoid looking inward and gaining insight into their own motivations and emotions because they are afraid of introspection and critical self-reflection. In this case, increasing self-awareness can assist the individual in comprehending their influence on others and making adjustments to enhance their relationships with friends and family. This can be accomplished by practicing mindfulness, getting feedback from others, and reflecting on oneself. A person can better comprehend their thoughts, feelings, and actions with increased self-awareness, allowing them to make positive life adjustments.

In conclusion, a person's relationships, well-being, and success can all be negatively impacted by a lack of self-awareness. However, individuals can gain a deeper comprehension of their thoughts, feelings, and actions by enhancing self-awareness through therapy, self-reflection, and seeking feedback from others. Personal development, enhanced relationships, and increased life satisfaction may result from this.

It is essential to keep in mind that developing self-awareness is not a one-time event; rather, it is a never-ending process of growth and development. People can continue to increase their self-awareness and make positive changes in their lives by consistently reflecting on themselves and seeking feedback from others.

In a nutshell, a person's potential can be limited by a lack of self-awareness; however, gaining self-awareness gives them the tools they need to lead a life that is more meaningful and fulfilling.

10.Negative Mindset

Negative attitude is characterized by a recurring way of thinking that emphasizes the negative parts of life and views problems and challenges as insurmountable. Negative thinkers frequently possess a pessimistic view and feel unable to alter their situation. They could obsess over the past and worry unnecessarily about the future, which makes them feel helpless and hopeless. A gloomy outlook can have a variety of effects on a person's life. It may result in low confidence and self-esteem, which makes it challenging to pursue objectives and try new things. Stress, anxiety, and sadness can result from it, which can also have an impact on a person's physical and mental health.

It might be challenging to change one's perspective to one that is more positive and optimistic, but it is possible to do so with effort and persistence. This can entail engaging in activities that encourage positive thinking and well-being, expressing appreciation, and practicing mindfulness. It can also entail asking friends and family for help. People with a negative mindset can increase their overall happiness and quality of life by altering the way they view themselves and their lives.

There are various causes of a negative psychology, containing:

a. Childhood experiences: A frightening or troublesome childhood, containing experiences in the way that abuse, neglect, or want, can bring about a negative psychology.
b. Brain allure: Some individuals grant permission to resort to bad attitude on account of their brain allure and neurobiological determinants.
c. Social and enlightening determinants: Living in negative or stressful surroundings, or being unprotected to negative ideas in the news, can cause a negative mindset.
d. Personal happenings: Negative knowledge in the way that misfortune, trauma, or misstep can bring about a negative

psychology, specifically if one believes they are being the reason for these occurrences.

e. Mental strength issues: Mental fitness conditions to a degree worry or concavity can bring about negative thinking and a determined gloomy view.
f. Chronic stress: Prolonged stress and uncovering difficult events can bring about a negative psychology, in addition to material and mental energy questions.

It should be noted that negative attitudes can also be sustained, leading to a vicious cycle of negative thoughts. By recognizing and addressing the underlying causes, people can strive to shift to a more positive and optimistic attitude.

There are a few systems that can assist people with beating a pessimistic mentality and foster a more uplifting perspective on life, including:

a. Challenge negative contemplations: Becoming mindful of negative considerations and testing them with proof and levelheaded reasoning can help shift towards a more certain mentality.
b. Gratitude Practice: Zeroing in on what one is thankful for and developing a demeanor of appreciation can assist with moving consideration away from negative contemplations and towards the positive parts of life.
c. Physical activity engagement: Exercise has been displayed to emphatically affect temperament and emotional wellness and can help shift towards a more certain mentality.
d. Associating with others: Building and keeping up with positive associations with companions, family, and friends and family can offer help and neutralize negative reasoning.
e. Participating in care and contemplation: Care practices can assist people with turning out to be more mindful of their

viewpoints and feelings and foster a more uplifting perspective
on life.

f. Looking for proficient assistance: If negative reasoning is persevering and influencing day to day existence, looking for the assistance of an emotional wellness expert can be valuable.

It is essential to recollect that having an impact on a negative mentality is a cycle, and it requires investment and exertion. Nonetheless, with perseverance and commitment, people can defeat pessimistic reasoning and carry on with a seriously satisfying and positive life.

Someone who has had a career setback, such as losing their job or being promoted, might be a real-world illustration of a negative mindset. This individual may begin to believe that they are incapable of success and begin to view themselves as a failure. They might also begin to focus on the bad aspects of their life and ignore the good, beginning to see the world as hostile and hostile.

They may experience feelings of hopelessness, defeat, and lack of motivation because of this negative outlook on life. They might withdraw from social activities and relationships rather than taking risks or looking for new opportunities. As a result of their negative thinking, they may also experience an increase in levels of stress, anxiety, and depression.

This individual, on the other hand, has the potential to transform into a more upbeat person with the right strategies and support. For instance, they might begin by recognizing and combating their negative thoughts, focusing on the things for which they are grateful, and getting some exercise. To overcome their negative thoughts and cultivate a more upbeat outlook on life, they may also seek assistance from friends, family, or a mental health professional.

In conclusion, a negative attitude can significantly affect a person's life and health. It can make people feel hopeless, make them less motivated, and make them less happy with life. However, it is possible to overcome a pessimistic outlook and cultivate a more upbeat attitude. Defeating negative thoughts, cultivating gratitude, engaging in physical activity, connecting with others, practicing mindfulness and meditation, and seeking professional assistance if necessary are all examples of this.

It is essential to keep in mind that overcoming a negative mindset requires time, effort, patience, and persistence. However, individuals can overcome negative thinking and lead lives that are more satisfying and positive with dedication and a commitment to personal development and well-being.

A friend or acquaintance who consistently sees the glass as half empty might serve as an actual illustration of someone who has a pessimistic mentality. They might, for instance, place a greater emphasis on the potential drawbacks and challenges than on the advantages and possibilities when presented with an opportunity. They might also be quick to lament the things going on in their lives, like their job, relationships, and financial situation.

Additionally, they might have trouble seeing the positive aspects of their lives and instead concentrate on the negative aspects. For instance, rather than accepting compliments and feeling proud of their accomplishments, they may dismiss them or downplay their significance.

Because their negativity can be contagious and affect the moods and attitudes of those around them, it can be difficult to be in their company. However, it is essential to approach these people with empathy, comprehension, and an eagerness to assist. It is possible to assist them in developing a more upbeat outlook on life by providing support and encouraging them to concentrate on the positive aspects of their lives.

11.Lack of Focus

Lack of focus is the inability to focus on a task, goal, or objective and give it the attention it deserves in life. As a result, people may experience feelings of confusion, frustration, and overwhelm as they are unable to move forward and achieve their goals. Distractions, a lack of motivation, poor time management, a lack of clear goals or priorities, high levels of stress or anxiety, and other factors can all contribute to a lack of focus in life. A general sense of being stuck, difficulty completing tasks, and lower productivity are all possible outcomes of this.

It is essential to identify the underlying causes of lack of focus and develop strategies to address them to overcome it in life. This might entail establishing precise objectives, devising a strategy to set priorities for tasks, minimizing distractions, putting stress-management strategies into practice, and seeking assistance when necessary. People can regain control of their attention and move closer to the things that matter most to them by taking a focused and deliberate approach.

Lack of focus in life can be caused by a number of things, some of which are:

a. Distractions: It can be difficult to focus on a task because of the constant inundation of information and the environment and technology.
b. A lack of drive: It's hard to focus and put in the effort needed when you don't want to do something.
c. Ineffective time management skills: Having trouble effectively managing your time can make it hard to prioritize tasks and feel overwhelmed.
d. Absence of clear objectives or priorities: It can be hard to focus and move forward if you don't know exactly what you want to accomplish.
e. Anxiety or stress levels that are high: Concentration and

productivity can be difficult to achieve when you are under stress or anxiety.

f. Not enough sleep: Lack of sleep can affect concentration, output, and well-being.
g. Negative mental or physical health: Focus and overall well-being can be negatively impacted by chronic physical or mental health conditions.
h. Addiction to drugs: Focus and overall well-being can be impacted by drug or alcohol use.

There may also be other factors at play, but these are some of the most common causes of life focuslessness. It is essential to identify the underlying causes of lack of focus and develop strategies to address them to overcome it.

There are several ways to deal with life's lack of focus, some of which include:

a. Finding sources of distraction: Take steps to reduce or eliminate any distractions that are interfering with your ability to concentrate.
b. Prioritizing and defining clear objectives: Make sure you know exactly what you want to accomplish and put your tasks in order of importance.
c. Enhancing skills in time management: Improve your time management skills to reduce feelings of being overwhelmed.
d. Mindfulness training: Be in the now and pay attention to your thoughts and emotions. Focus can be improved, and stress and anxiety can be reduced by this.
e. Getting sufficient sleep: Getting 7-9 hours of sleep each night will help you focus better and feel better overall.
f. Enhancing mental and physical well-being: If you're having problems with your physical or mental health, you should exercise regularly, eat a healthy diet, and seek support.

g. Abstaining from substance use: Do not consume alcohol or drugs because they can impair concentration and general well-being.
h. Getting help: If you're having trouble staying focused, don't be afraid to ask for help. For support and direction, talk to a trusted friend, family member, or therapist.

You can sharpen your focus and move closer to achieving your goals by putting these methods into practice.

Someone who has trouble focusing on their work is an example of someone who lacks focus in life. It may be hard for them to get back to their work after being interrupted by emails, phone notifications, or other things. This can result in lower levels of output, missed deadlines, and a general sense of frustration and exhaustion.

Take, for instance, John, a software developer who has difficulty staying focused. Emails and notifications from social media frequently distract him, despite his best efforts. He struggles to stay on task as a result, and he frequently feels overwhelmed by the amount of work he must do. John is aware that his inability to concentrate is a problem, but he does not know how to fix it.

John could try implementing some of the previously mentioned solutions, such as reducing distractions, setting clear goals and priorities, and practicing mindfulness, to address his lack of focus. He could also get help from a mentor or therapist to learn more about his tendencies and come up with a strategy to make him more focused and productive.

Finally, I'd like to stress that while a lack of focus can be a long-lasting and crippling problem, it is also one that most people can control. People can overcome this obstacle and improve their ability to concentrate, stay on task, and achieve their goals by understanding the causes and implementing practical solutions.

It is essential to keep in mind that becoming more focused and productive takes a lifetime and may not be achieved overnight. However, anyone can make significant advancements in this area with perseverance and dedication.

Being kind to oneself and recognize that failures are a normal part of the process are also important. When faced with difficulties, it is essential to acknowledge one's emotions and, if necessary, seek assistance from friends, family, or a mental health professional.

In the end, having a sense of focus and direction in life can help people reach their full potential and provide a sense of purpose and fulfillment. Therefore, if you are having trouble staying focused, I urge you to act, seek assistance, and persevere in your efforts to improve.

12.Lack of Discipline

Lack of discipline is the inability to maintain consistency and focus in one's behavior or actions in life. It can show up in a variety of ways, like not taking care of responsibilities, not sticking to routines or schedules, and having trouble moving toward personal or professional goals. It may be challenging for people who lack discipline to effectively set and achieve goals, prioritize tasks, and manage their time. Additionally, they may have difficulty exercising self-control and finding it difficult to resist temptations or distractions that could impede their efforts.

Lack of discipline can be brought on by a variety of factors, including a lack of motivation, unclear objectives, inability to handle stress, or a underlying mental health condition. However, it can be overcome with deliberate effort and self-discipline-promoting strategies. Setting clear and attainable goals, creating a schedule or routine, practicing mindfulness, developing positive habits, avoiding distractions, seeking accountability and support from others, and rewarding oneself for good behavior are some effective strategies for overcoming lack of discipline. In conclusion, an individual's lack of discipline can hinder their personal and professional development as well as their performance in a variety of areas. However, individuals can cultivate the necessary self-discipline to achieve their goals and live a more satisfying life with the right strategies and support.

Life's lack of discipline can have a variety of complex and multifaceted causes. Lack of discipline is frequently brought on by:

a. lack of understanding of goals: It's possible that people won't be able to maintain their discipline if they don't know what they want. People may have trouble staying focused and motivated if they don't have a clear idea of what they want to accomplish.

b. Procrastination: The practice of delaying or postponing tasks is known as procrastination, and it can result in a lack of discipline. It may be challenging for people to refocus and get back on track if they consistently put off important tasks.
c. Aversion to failure: People may avoid acting or making decisions out of fear of failure. Individuals may lack the self-assurance and drive necessary to maintain discipline when they are afraid of failing.
d. Overwhelm and stress: Overwhelm and stress can make it hard for people to be disciplined. It can be hard for people to stay focused and more likely to be distracted when they are under a lot of stress or overwhelmed.
e. Insufficient accountability: It's possible that people won't be motivated to keep their discipline when they aren't held accountable for their actions. People may find it easier to give in to temptation or procrastinate when they don't have someone to answer or give feedback to.
f. Lack of self-control: It may be difficult for some people to exercise self-control and to avoid being distracted or tempted. It may be difficult for people who lack self-control to maintain discipline in their actions or behavior.
g. Conditions underlying mental health: People who suffer from mental health conditions like depression or anxiety may find it difficult to maintain their discipline. It's possible that people who are struggling with mental health issues lack the drive or vitality necessary to maintain focus and discipline.

In conclusion, a lack of discipline in life can be caused by a variety of factors, including stress and overwhelm on the outside and anxiety and lack of motivation on the inside. People can develop strategies to overcome them and cultivate the necessary discipline to achieve their goals by comprehending the underlying causes.

There are many ways to deal with life's lack of discipline. The following are some possible approaches that might help:

a. Clearly define your goals: People can stay focused and motivated by setting clear and specific goals. It might be simpler for people to maintain their discipline and work toward their objectives if they have a crystal-clear idea of what they want to accomplish.
b. Establish a routine and schedule: People can gain a sense of structure and consistency in their daily lives by developing a routine and schedule. People may find it easier to maintain discipline and avoid distractions when they have a set routine.
c. Make use of reinforcement: Rewarding oneself for achieving goals or remaining disciplined is known as positive reinforcement. This can help people stay on track and be a powerful motivator.
d. Make time for yourself: Self-care can help people feel less stressed and have more energy overall. It may be easier for people to keep their focus and discipline when they take care of their physical and mental health.
e. Make yourself accountable: People can stay motivated and on track by asking a friend, family member, or mentor to hold them accountable. People may be able to maintain their discipline and receive a sense of external motivation from having someone to answer to.
f. Divide tasks into smaller, easier-to-manage steps: People can avoid feeling overwhelmed or discouraged by breaking down larger tasks into smaller, more manageable steps. It might be simpler for people to maintain their discipline and make progress toward their objectives if they concentrate on smaller, more manageable steps.
g. Find and address the root causes: If underlying issues like depression, anxiety, or low self-esteem are connected to lack of discipline, it may be necessary to directly address these

issues. In this regard, seeking support from a therapist or counselor may be beneficial.

In conclusion, there are several approaches people can take to deal with life's lack of discipline. An important part of the process can be experimenting with various strategies to determine which one is most effective for you. A lack of discipline can be overcome, and goals can be achieved with dedication and persistence.

A person who lacks discipline in life is like this:

Johan is a young adult who has had trouble keeping order in his life. He has a lot of goals, but it's hard for him to stay focused and motivated. He procrastinates frequently and struggles with time management, frequently being distracted by friends, social media, or television. He struggles to catch up on his work because he frequently misses deadlines. Johan's lack of discipline is stressing him out and making it hard for him to reach his goals. He is aware that he needs to make some adjustments to his life, but he is overwhelmed and doesn't know where to begin. He has attempted to create plans and schedules in the past, but they never seem to stick. Johan starts by setting clear and specific goals for himself to address his lack of discipline. He decides to concentrate on finishing a project he has put off for weeks. He creates a schedule for completing each step and divides the project into smaller, more manageable steps. Johan uses positive reinforcement to help him keep his discipline by rewarding himself with small treats or activities after completing each step. He also asks a friend to hold him accountable, who monitors his progress and encourages him to stay on course.

John is able to complete his project on time and with greater ease by employing these methods. He learns the importance of clearly defining objectives, developing routines, and remaining accountable. He is able to remain disciplined throughout his life and advance toward his other objectives over time.

One more example of lack of discipline is of a student who frequently procrastinates and struggles to complete assignments on time. The student may have trouble staying focused on studies and frequently become involved in games, social media, or other activities. The student might put off studying until the very last minute, which could lead to work of lower quality or missed deadlines. The student's academic performance and stress may be negatively impacted by this lack of discipline. The student may continue to struggle and face negative consequences in both the academic and personal lives if they do not make changes and implement strategies to improve their discipline.

One's progress and success in life can be hampered by a lack of discipline. It may result in procrastination, missed opportunities, and poor decision-making, all of which can have a negative impact on both one's personal and professional lives. As a result, it's critical to identify and address the underlying causes of poor discipline.

The good news is that discipline is a skill that can be acquired through effort and practice over time. When it comes to creating routines and habits, it takes self-awareness, drive, and consistency. One can establish a sense of discipline and control in their life by establishing clear goals, breaking them down into manageable steps, and developing a strategy for achieving them.

It is essential to keep in mind that cultivating discipline is not an easy task, and failures and difficulties will invariably occur. However, these challenges can be overcome, and success can be achieved in all areas of life with persistence and dedication.

13.Lack of Consistency

Lack of consistency in life is a situation in which there is a lack of regularity, predictability, or stability in one's thoughts, actions, or circumstances. To put it another way, it is a state in which one's behavior, actions, or outcomes are erratic or unpredictable. This lack of consistency can show up in work, relationships, health, personal habits, and other areas of life. A lack of consistency in personal habits, on the other hand, may manifest as an inability to adhere to a healthy eating or exercise routine, while a lack of consistency in work may manifest as erratic attendance or an inability to meet deadlines.

Uncertainty and instability brought on by the lack of consistency can also result in tension and worry. It may also affect one's capacity to realize long-term objectives and desires, as success frequently depends on consistency. In general, inconsistent behavior can have a negative impact on a variety of aspects of life and pose a significant barrier to personal and professional development. As a result, it is necessary to pinpoint the areas in which consistency is lacking and to take steps to rectify these issues.

Life's lack of consistency can be caused by many things. Some of the most typical reasons are as follows:

a. Lack of motivation: It can be difficult for someone who lacks motivation to maintain consistent behavior or exert effort toward achieving their objectives.
b. Poor Time Management: Inconsistency in many areas of life, including relationships, work, and personal habits, can result from poor time management.
c. Absence of focus: It may be difficult for someone who lacks focus to maintain consistency in their personal or professional lives.

d. Aversion to failure: Because they are afraid of failing or making mistakes, some people may avoid consistently pursuing their goals.
e. Personal difficulties: A person may have trouble staying consistent in a variety of areas of their life due to personal obstacles like chronic illness or mental health issues.
f. External variables: A person's routine can be disrupted by external factors, such as changes in circumstances or unanticipated occurrences, which can result in a lack of consistency.
g. Lack of accountability: A person may have trouble staying consistent in their actions or efforts toward achieving their goals if they are not held accountable.

To effectively address a lack of consistency, it is essential to identify its root causes. Setting clear goals and priorities, addressing personal challenges, developing effective time management skills, and seeking support or accountability from others are all examples of this.

There are several ways to deal with and get over life's lack of consistency. The following are some possible solutions:

a. Setting clear goals: Providing direction and focus can be helped by setting clear, attainable goals. People are more likely to remain consistent in their efforts to achieve their goals when they have a clear idea of what they want to accomplish.
b. Dividing goals into smaller achievable steps: It is possible to avoid feeling overwhelmed and to feel like you are making progress by dividing larger objectives into smaller, more manageable tasks. Additionally, this can assist in making the undertaking appear less difficult and increase the likelihood of consistency.

c. Establishing a routine: It can be easier to stay on track and help form habits by establishing a regular routine. A routine or schedule that includes time for work, exercise, self-care, and leisure activities can be helpful.
d. Be accountable and use reminders: Accountability and reminders can help people stay on track and avoid falling back into old ways of doing things. This can be done by setting reminders on a computer or phone or by finding an accountability partner with whom you can regularly check in.
e. Practicing self-compassion: When trying to be consistent, it's important to be kind to oneself. Accept that there may be lapses in consistency or setbacks, but don't let them stop progress.

One can cultivate and bolster the habit of completing tasks and achieving goals by implementing these strategies and remaining committed to consistency. This may, over time, result in a greater sense of accomplishment, increased output, and a life that is more satisfying.

Let's look at Tom, a man who has trouble maintaining consistency in his professional life.

Tom works as a software engineer, but he frequently has trouble meeting deadlines or finishing work on time. He may be enthusiastic and energetic at the beginning of a project, but over time he loses focus and motivation. When he is motivated, he tends to work in short bursts, completing tasks quickly and effectively, but when the excitement wears off, he loses momentum. Consequently, Tom frequently misses deadlines, which can be problematic for his team and business. Tom still has trouble sticking to his manager's repeated reminders about the significance of meeting deadlines and being consistent in his work.

Tom's professional life may be affected in multiple ways by this lack of consistency. His coworkers might begin to think of him as unreliable, which could hurt his name and make it harder for him to work well as a team member. His manager might lose faith in his ability to finish projects, which could influence his career development and opportunities for promotion. Tom, on the other hand, can work on devising plans to boost his consistency and follow-through. He can, for instance, break down his tasks into smaller, easier-to-manage steps and set himself goals that are doable. He can also make a routine or schedule that helps him stay focused and on track. In addition, he may be able to develop the skills and routines necessary for greater consistency in his work if he seeks assistance from his manager or a mentor.

Our personal and professional goals, as well as other aspects of our lives, can be negatively impacted by lack of consistency. It can be challenging to achieve our goals, cultivate healthy relationships, and form positive habits if we are inconsistent. It can also result in feelings of anger, dejection, and even failure.

However, it is essential to keep in mind that consistency is a skill that can be acquired and refined over time. We can cultivate greater discipline and follow-through in our lives by determining the root causes of our inconsistent behavior and taking deliberate steps to address them.

Setting clear goals, making a schedule or routine, breaking larger tasks down into smaller steps, getting help from others, and practicing self-discipline and self-motivation are all good ways to build consistency. We can develop the habits and mindset necessary to achieve our goals and lead lives that are more satisfying and successful with consistent effort and practice.

14. Lack of Perseverance

Lack of perseverance in life is characterized by the inability of a person to keep working towards their objectives in the face of obstacles or disappointments. A lack of confidence, willpower, and perseverance to persist in the face of challenges characterizes this mentality. Because it enables a person to overcome obstacles, gain knowledge from mistakes, and accomplish their objectives, perseverance is an essential quality for success in numerous spheres of life. A person's inability to persevere can make it difficult for them to realize their goals and cause them to feel disappointed and frustrated.

Perseverance difficulties can arise for a variety of reasons. It could be because of a lack of confidence in oneself, a lack of motivation, or a fear of failing. A person's inability to effectively manage their time, a lack of support from others, or a lack of direction or clarity regarding their goals are additional factors that can contribute to a lack of perseverance. To achieve personal and professional development, it is essential to address a lack of perseverance. This could mean coming up with ways to stay motivated, getting help from others, practicing self-care and reflection, and learning from mistakes and setbacks. No matter how difficult the journey is, anyone can overcome obstacles and achieve their goals with perseverance and determination.

In life, a lack of perseverance can have many different manifestations. Below is the list of few common ones:

a. Aversion to failure: A lack of perseverance is frequently brought on by a fear of failing. Even when they are capable, a person may avoid taking risks or working toward their goals when they are afraid of failing.
b. Lack of motivation: It can be difficult for someone to keep working toward their goals if they lack motivation. It can be hard for someone to stay committed to their goals if they don't have a clear sense of purpose or inspiration.
c. Adverse self-talk: Negative self-talk can make it hard to keep

going. A person may have trouble staying motivated, doubt their abilities, and feel discouraged by setbacks when they have a negative self-image or mentality.

d. Lack of assistance: A person's ability to persevere can be hampered by a lack of support from others. A person's motivation may be difficult to maintain, and they may be more likely to give up when they feel alone or unsupported in their efforts.
e. Lack of guidance: It may be difficult for someone to remain persistent without a clear sense of direction or purpose. A person may feel overwhelmed or discouraged and be more likely to give up when they are unsure of their goals or how to achieve them.
f. Personal difficulties: Perseverance can be difficult to maintain due to personal obstacles like mental health issues or chronic illness. It can be hard to stay motivated and committed to achieving goals when faced with these obstacles, which can be draining.

To effectively address a lack of perseverance, it is essential to identify its root causes. Setting realistic goals and expectations, practicing self-reflection and self-care, developing strategies to remain motivated, and seeking support and direction from others are all examples of this.

It can be difficult to deal with a lack of perseverance, but there are few ways to deal with it that can work. To deal with a lack of perseverance in life, some possible solutions include:

a. Setting specific and achievable goals: A sense of purpose and direction can be gained by setting goals that are specific and attainable. A person may be more motivated to persevere in their efforts when they have clear objectives to work toward.
b. Divide tasks into manageable steps: It can be easier to stay focused and avoid feeling overwhelmed when larger tasks or goals are broken down into smaller, more manageable steps.

In the face of obstacles, this can assist in maintaining motivation and perseverance.

c. Create a positive attitude: Positive self-talk and cultivating a positive mindset can help people overcome doubts and negative thoughts that may be holding them back. Reframing setbacks as opportunities for growth and concentrating on one's strengths, accomplishments, and progress is one way to accomplish this.
d. Obtain assistance and accountability: When it comes to sustaining perseverance, asking for help and direction from other people can be a useful resource. Participating in a community of support, joining a mentorship or advice group, or working with a coach or therapist to create a strategy for overcoming obstacles are all examples of this.
e. Make time for yourself: Taking care of oneself can be a crucial part of staying persistent. Engaging in activities that bring joy and fulfillment, getting enough rest and exercise, adhering to a healthy diet, and practicing mindfulness or meditation are all examples of this.
f. Learn from Failures and setbacks: Resilience and perseverance can be strengthened by learning from setbacks and failures. This might entail pondering what went wrong, determining what could have been done differently in the future, and making use of these experiences as a chance to grow and learn.

A person can increase their perseverance and overcome obstacles to achieve their goals by implementing these strategies. It is essential to keep in mind that while developing perseverance requires time and effort, it is doable with dedication and practice.

Someone who desires to learn a new language but quickly gives up after encountering initial obstacles is an illustration of a person who lacks perseverance in life. Let's go by the name "Amy."

Amy decides that she wants to learn French because she wants to visit France one day and has always been interested in French culture. She enrolls in a French beginner's course and begins learning the language. However, after a few weeks, the grammar and pronunciation rules started to frustrate and overwhelm her. She stops practicing at home and starts missing classes. Amy starts to doubt her ability to learn French after a few weeks. She is discouraged because she believes she might not be suited to learning languages. She eventually decides that learning French is not worth the effort and gives up completely.

Several factors contribute to Amy's lack of perseverance in this instance. It's possible that she wasn't motivated or that she didn't know where she was going with her language learning. The initial difficulties and setbacks that come with learning a new language may have also discouraged her.

Amy could employ several strategies to address this lack of perseverance. She could begin by breaking down her goals for learning a language into smaller, more manageable steps, like learning a few new words from the vocabulary each day. She could also seek assistance from a language partner or tutor for additional accountability and support. Finally, rather than dwelling on setbacks or failures, she could work on cultivating a more upbeat outlook by focusing on her progress and accomplishments.

Amy could overcome her lack of perseverance and keep working toward her goal of learning French by implementing these strategies. She could fulfill her dream of traveling to France and become fluent in the language with dedication and perseverance.

People can face significant difficulties in life if they lack perseverance because it can prevent them from achieving their objectives and realizing their potential. However, it is essential to keep in mind that perseverance is a skill that can be acquired through effort and practice over time.

A lack of perseverance can be caused by several things, including a negative attitude, unclear objectives, and a lack of motivation. Setting attainable goals, breaking tasks down into manageable steps, seeking support and accountability, and practicing self-care are all strategies that can help overcome these challenges.

In the end, perseverance can only be developed by being willing to persevere and overcome obstacles. It requires self-confidence and a commitment to learning and development. Developing perseverance can be extremely rewarding and empowering, leading to greater success and fulfillment in all aspects of life, even though it can be a challenging and occasionally frustrating journey.

15.Lack of Patience

LIfe's lack of patience is the inability or difficulty of enduring delay, challenges, or adversity. When things don't happen as quickly or easily as expected, it causes agitation, frustration, and irritation. It can be difficult for people who lack patience to wait for results, accomplish long-term objectives, or deal with difficult situations. Working relationships, personal goals, and other areas of life can all be affected by a lack of patience. A person who lacks patience, for instance, may have trouble working on a project that takes a lot of time and effort, or they may become easily agitated when their partner does not respond to a text message in a timely manner. They may become impatient with the sluggish progress they see in losing weight or gaining muscle, which may make it difficult for them to maintain a healthy lifestyle. High expectations, perfectionism, and a need for control are all potential causes of a lack of patience. It can also be influenced by societal factors like the demand for quick results and the prevalence of instant gratification.

It's important to remember that patience is a skill that can be learned and honed over time, even though it can be frustrating to have a lack of it. It necessitates a willingness to accept uncertainty, surrender control, and concentrate on the here and now. People can become more patient and resilient in the face of challenges if they practice mindfulness, set realistic expectations, and reframe challenges as opportunities for growth.

A lack of patience in life can be caused by several things. Typical reasons include:

a. Expectations too high: Because they want things to happen quickly and in accordance with their own vision, people who have high expectations frequently have difficulty showing patience. They might become irritated and impatient if things don't work out the way they planned.
b. Perfectionism: Because they are focused on completing tasks

flawlessly and quickly, perfectionists may struggle with patience. When they believe that progress is too sluggish or that they experience setbacks, they may become impatient with themselves or others.

c. Control needs: When things or outcomes are out of their control, people who need to feel in control can become impatient. They might feel helpless and frustrated, which might cause them to be impatient and restless.
d. Anxiety and stress: Because these conditions can make you feel more restless and irritable, stress and anxiety can make it hard to be patient. People may think they don't have time or energy to wait for things to happen when they are stressed.
e. Instant gratification culture: It can be challenging to cultivate patience in a society that places a high value on instant gratification. We are accustomed to having quick and easy access to information, goods, and services, which can lead us to have unreasonable expectations regarding how quickly things should occur.
f. Character traits: It's possible that some people simply have a personality that is more impulsive, impatient, or restless than others. Being patient and waiting for results can be more difficult due to these personality traits.

It's important to remember that different people have different reasons for being impatient, and that sometimes there may be more than one factor at play. However, individuals can work to increase their patience and resilience in the face of challenges by determining the root causes of impatience.

People can improve their patience and control their impatience through a variety of methods. The following are some possible strategies for dealing with life's lack of patience:

a. Practicing mindfulness: Being mindful means being completely present and aware of the present moment. People can learn to be more patient and tolerant of the present moment, even when it is not exactly how they would like it to be, by regularly engaging in mindfulness practice.

b. Be realistic about your goals: Frustration and impatience can result from unrealistic expectations. People can better manage their impatience and appreciate the progress they are making by setting realistic goals and expectations.
c. Make gratitude a habit: People can focus on the good things in their lives and appreciate what they already have with the assistance of gratitude. People can be more patient and receptive to their current circumstance if they focus on their gratitude.
d. Rethink obstacles as opportunities: Recasting difficulties and setbacks as opportunities for development and learning can be helpful. People may be able to work through challenging situations with greater patience and persistence with the assistance of this perspective.
e. Concentrate on the process: People can concentrate on the process of achieving their objectives rather than just the result. People can appreciate the progress they are making and be more patient with the time it takes to achieve their goals by focusing on the process and the steps involved.
f. Taking breaks: People can recharge and return to a task with a new perspective by taking breaks. People can control their impatience and avoid feeling overwhelmed or frustrated by taking breaks.

In general, cultivating greater patience necessitates a willingness to engage in mindfulness practice, establish expectations that are attainable, and view difficulties as opportunities for development. People can learn to be more patient and resilient in the face of challenges if they put in the effort on a regular basis.

Consider Nathan, a person who might lack patience in a variety of situations. For instance, Nathan might quickly lose his cool and grow angry while dealing with delayed customer service or lengthy lineups at a store. Also, he can have problems waiting for others to complete speaking or he might interrupt others to share his opinions.

When Nathan is learning a new skill, like a new language or musical instrument, he may exhibit a lack of patience. When progress seems to be slow, Nathan might become impatient, and it might be hard for him to stay motivated when he doesn't see results right away. He may become dissatisfied with himself for not being able to quickly master the skill, which may cause him to give up on the endeavor altogether.

In this instance, Nathan's lack of patience could be caused by a fear of failing or a desire for immediate gratification. It's possible that he has a hard time accepting the idea that learning a new skill takes time and effort because he is used to seeing results immediately in other areas of his life. Additionally, he may be reluctant to practice and put in the necessary effort to improve due to his fear of making mistakes or appearing foolish in front of others.

Nathan might benefit from changing his perspective and concentrating on the learning process rather than the end result in order to address his lack of patience. It could also be beneficial for him to break the skill down into smaller, more manageable steps and to reward himself for completing each step. Even when progress appears to be slow, this may assist him in remaining motivated and experiencing a sense of progress.

All in all, absence of persistence can essentially affect an individual's life, influencing their capacity to master new abilities, oversee pressure, and keep up with solid connections. People like Nathan can develop greater patience and resilience in the face of challenges in life by recognizing the root causes of impatience and practicing strategies to manage it.

Being impatient can be difficult in life since it can cause stress, frustration, and even missed opportunities. However, it's crucial to keep in mind that patience is a trait that can be honed and improved with practice. People can learn to control their impatience and develop stronger resilience in the face of difficulties with effort and determination.

The fact that impatience can have both internal and external reasons, such as exaggerated expectations, a need for rapid fulfillment, or external pressures, must also be acknowledged. People can attempt to address the underlying reasons for impatience and create better-coping mechanisms by figuring out what those causes are.

In the end, committing to personal development and improvement is necessary to cultivate greater patience. Individuals can develop greater patience and resilience in all aspects of their lives by engaging in mindfulness, setting reasonable expectations, and reframing challenges as opportunities for growth.

16.Lack of Time Management

Lack of time management refers to a person's inability to efficiently divide their time between the various responsibilities and pursuits in their life. This may appear as a sensation of overwhelm or perpetual busyness, as well as a sense of not being able to finish everything they need to in the time allotted. People who have trouble managing their time might always be late, miss deadlines, and feel stressed and anxious. A sense of disorganization and chaos in their lives may result from their inability to prioritize their responsibilities and establish attainable goals for themselves.

Procrastination, poor planning, a lack of prioritization, and an inability to say no to requests or demands on their time are some of the causes of a lack of time management. A lack of self-discipline and concentration can also play a role, as can other forms of entertainment or distractions like social media. Overall, poor time management can result in missed opportunities, strained relationships, and more stress and anxiety. However, it is possible to improve one's time management skills and increase productivity, success, and happiness in life with the right strategies and tools.

A variety of distinct factors might contribute to poor time management in daily life. Typical explanations include:

a. Procrastination: A lack of time management can result from delaying tasks until the last minute. People who struggle with procrastination frequently find that they must rush to complete tasks at the last minute, which can lead to anxiety and stress.
b. Poor planning: Disorganization and a lack of prioritization can result from failing to plan out activities and tasks. It's easy to get sidetracked or distracted by other things if you don't have a clear plan.
c. Overcommitment: A lack of time management can result from accepting an excessive number of requests or demands on one's time. When attempting to manage multiple

commitments at once, those who struggle with overcommitment frequently find themselves stretched to breaking point.

d. Distractions: A lack of time management can be exacerbated by distractions like television, social media, and other forms of entertainment.
e. Absence of focus: A lack of time management can also be caused by difficulties concentrating and staying focused on the task at hand. People who have trouble staying focused may have trouble finishing tasks on time or being easily distracted.
f. System inefficiencies: A lack of time management can be caused by ineffective time management systems or tools, such as an unorganized calendar or to-do list. It can be challenging to effectively prioritize and track tasks without an efficient system in place.

Individuals can identify the areas in which they struggle and develop strategies to improve their time management skills by understanding the causes of a lack of time management.

Individuals can overcome a lack of time management and improve their time management skills through a variety of strategies. The following are some possible solutions:

a. Set clear objectives: Setting clear goals is one of the most crucial steps in effective time management. Make a list of your top priorities and set definite, attainable objectives for what you want to accomplish.
b. Prioritize your work: Learn to rank your work according to how important and urgent it is. You can get assistance deciding which tasks to focus on first by making use of tools like the ABC method or the Eisenhower Matrix.

c. Establish a schedule: Create a schedule for your day or week using a planner or calendar, with times set aside for activities. To stay on track, adhere to your schedule as closely as you can.
d. Reduce distractions: Find the things that keep you from your work and try to keep them to a minimum. This could entail closing your email, turning off your phone, or finding a quiet place to work.
e. Be able to say no: It is essential to acquire the ability to decline requests for your time that are beyond your capacity. Prioritize your own objectives and responsibilities and establish clear boundaries.
f. Take breaks: Taking breaks throughout the day can help you focus and work more efficiently. Make time for brief breaks to rest and refuel your body and mind.
g. Learn to delegate task: When possible, learn to delegate tasks to others, particularly those that are less important or can be completed by someone else.

Keep in mind that developing effective time management is a skill that requires consistent practice and hard work. To improve your time management skills and have greater success in your personal and professional lives, start with small changes and build on your success.

Abigail is someone who struggles with time management. Let's look at how Abigail might be affected by a lack of time management. Abigail is a professional who is always working and has a lot to do. She is involved in several volunteer organizations in her community in addition to holding a demanding job that requires her to manage multiple projects and adhere to strict deadlines. Abigail frequently experiences feelings of overwhelm and stress because of the numerous demands placed on her time, despite her best efforts. Abigail's tendency to overcommit is one of the main reasons she doesn't know how to manage her time. She finds that she takes on more than she can handle and has trouble saying no to requests for her time.

Consequently, she frequently finds herself hurrying to complete tasks at the last minute, which can result in errors and subpar work.

Abigail's inability to prioritize tasks is another factor that contributes to her lack of time management skills. She often finds that instead of focusing on the tasks that are most urgent or important, she spends time on less important ones like checking email or scrolling through social media. Abigail may need to work on setting better time boundaries, learning to decline requests she cannot realistically handle, and better prioritizing her tasks to improve her time management skills. She might also benefit from making use of tools like a planner or a to-do list to keep her organized and focused on the things that matter most to her. Abigail can improve her time management skills and lessen her stress and overwhelm with practice and perseverance.

Time management skills are necessary for success in many areas of life, including work, school, personal relationships, and hobbies, in today's fast-paced world. Feelings of stress, overwhelm, and burnout can result from a lack of time management skills, as can a diminished capacity to accomplish one's objectives and fulfill one's responsibilities.

Setting clear goals, prioritizing tasks, delegating responsibilities, and making use of tools like planners and to-do lists are just a few of the many strategies and techniques that can assist individuals in improving their time management skills. Individuals must determine the specific factors that contribute to their inability to manage their time effectively and devise an individual strategy for addressing these issues.

People can reduce stress and overwhelm, increase productivity, and have greater success in their personal and professional lives by practicing effective time management skills. Mastering time management requires effort and dedication, but the rewards are well worth the effort.

17.Lack of Financial Management

Lack of financial management is the failure to successfully manage one's own money, including budgeting, saving, investing, and managing debt. Possible results include financial instability, debt, and a lack of financial security. Overspending, not saving enough for emergencies or retirement, taking on too much debt, or not properly managing credit are all examples of poor financial management. It could be brought on by a lack of financial education or literacy, poor financial planning, or simply a lack of discipline or willpower. People may find themselves living paycheck to paycheck, unable to meet their financial obligations to themselves and their families or establish a solid financial foundation. In extreme cases, financial crises like bankruptcy, foreclosure, or homelessness can result from poor financial management. Fortunately, there are a lot of options for improving one's financial management skills, such as online budgeting and money management tools, financial planning services, and personal finance courses. Anyone can improve their financial management skills and build a more secure financial future with education, discipline, and a willingness to learn and change.

Lack of financial management in life has several reasons, including:

a. Lack of financial education: Many people don't receive basic financial education in schools or at home, which can make it difficult for them to grasp how to handle money wisely.
b. Bad financial habits: Some people acquire very bad financial practices, such as excessive spending, living beyond their means, or failing to save money for the future or for emergencies.
c. Lack of financial planning: People may struggle to maximize their income and miss opportunities to save or invest if they do not have a clear plan for managing their finances.
d. Significant life events: It can be challenging to handle money successfully when major life events like job loss, divorce, or medical emergencies occur.

e. Financial setbacks: Expenses that you didn't anticipate, like car repairs or home repairs, can set you back financially and make it hard to stay on track with your financial goals.
f. Weak financial role models: It may be difficult for some people to acquire good financial management skills because they may grow up in households where poor financial habits or money management are the norm.
g. Mental health conditions: Conditions like depression or anxiety can make it challenging to successfully manage finances.

It's crucial to keep in mind that with time and effort, money management is a skill that can be acquired. People can overcome the obstacles to effective financial management and build a more secure financial future by looking for resources and education.

In life, poor financial management can be addressed in several ways, including:

a. Budgeting: An essential first step in managing one's personal finances is to create and adhere to a budget. People can better understand where their money is going and where they can cut back by keeping track of expenses and making a spending plan.
b. Saving: An important aspect of financial management is creating an emergency fund and saving for long-term financial objectives. Savings, even a small amount, can add up over time
and serve as a cushion against unforeseen costs.
c. Education in financial matters: Books, online courses, and financial planning services are just a few of the many options available to individuals looking to enhance their financial management abilities. Individuals can acquire the knowledge

and abilities necessary to effectively manage their finances by seeking education and advice.

d. Management of debt: Debt can be a significant obstacle to financial stability. People can lessen the burden of debt and improve their financial situation by devising a strategy for managing credit and paying off debt.
e. Getting professional assistance: Getting professional assistance from a credit counselor or financial planner can provide the direction and support needed to make positive changes for people who face significant financial difficulties.
f. Changing one's lifestyle: Changing one's spending habits, reducing expenses that aren't necessary, and sticking to one's budget are important changes to one's lifestyle that can help one manage their money better in the long run.

People can improve their financial security and stability for themselves and their families by practicing better financial management skills. It is essential to keep in mind that financial management is a process, and that progress may not be made immediately.

After completing her education, Tanya, 28, has just started her first job. Despite her high salary, she struggles to keep track of her finances. Her life is impacted in the following ways by her poor financial management:

a. Overspending: Tanya likes to splurge on entertainment, dining out, and shopping. However, she frequently spends more than she earns, leading to credit card debt.
b. Having no budget: Tanya does not budget or keep track of her expenses. She can't save money or make plans because it's hard for her to know where her money is going.
c. Inadequate financial preparation: Tanya hasn't given much thought to long-term financial objectives like buying a house, saving for a child's education, or retiring early. She has

difficulty aligning her financial decisions with her goals if she does not have a plan.

d. Impulsive decisions: When it comes to her finances, Tanya frequently acts irrationally, such as taking out a loan to purchase a new car or purchasing expensive items without considering the implications for her financial situation in the long run.
e. Poor credit control: Tanya has a low credit score and has missed payments on her credit card. This makes it harder for her to get credit in the future, which could make it harder for her to get a loan to buy a house or a car.

Tanya may benefit from consulting a credit counselor or financial planner to improve her financial situation. She could also make a budget and keep track of her expenses to see where her money is going. Finally, by paying her bills on time and paying down her debt, she could work to raise her credit score. Tanya can increase her financial security and stability by working on her financial management skills.

In conclusion, a lack of time management can result in a variety of negative life outcomes, including missing deadlines, experiencing more stress, being less productive, and not having a work-life balance. Internal or external factors, such as procrastination, distractions, or a full schedule, can contribute to poor time management. Setting priorities, creating a schedule, removing distractions, and learning to say "no" when necessary are all strategies and tools that can help improve time management skills. People can better manage their time and be more successful in their personal and professional lives by implementing these solutions. It is essential to keep in mind that improving one's ability to manage one's time effectively necessitates effort, perseverance, and dedication; however, the advantages of doing so are well worth the effort.

18.Lack of Communication

Lack of communication skills is the inability to effectively communicate and receive information verbally and nonverbally. Because they enable efficient collaboration, comprehension, and connection with others, communication skills are essential in both personal and professional relationships. People who aren't good at communicating may have trouble saying what they think and feeling confident, which can lead to misunderstandings and disagreements. They might also have trouble listening to other people and comprehending their points of view, which could make it hard for them to form meaningful relationships and work well in teams.

Speaking too quickly or too slowly, avoiding eye contact, interrupting other people, and failing to convey information clearly and concisely are all common indicators of poor communication skills. Social anxiety, cultural differences, and a lack of exposure to various communication styles are additional factors that can contribute to a lack of communication skills.

It's important to remember that practice and education can help improve communication skills. People can strengthen their relationships, advance in their careers, and achieve their personal goals by actively working to improve their communication skills.

Lack of communication skills can be caused by several things, including:

a. Lack of experience: To develop and improve communication skills require regular practice. It may be difficult for someone to express themselves clearly and effectively if they do not communicate frequently.
b. Social phobia: Social anxiety can make it hard for someone to talk to other people, make eye contact, or start a conversation.
c. Differing cultures: Culture-specific communication styles can be vastly different. Misunderstandings and breakdowns in communication can result when people from different cultural

backgrounds have difficulty understanding one another's communication style.

d. Learning disabilities: Learning disabilities, such as autism or attention deficit hyperactivity disorder (ADHD), may hinder a person's capacity for effective communication.
e. Lack of faith: Speaking to others can be hesitant and uncertain if you lack confidence. Being able to express oneself clearly and effectively can be challenging as a result.
f. Inadequate listening skills: It is essential to be a good speaker as well as a good listener to communicate effectively because it is a two-way process. People who have trouble listening to other people may have trouble comprehending their point of view and responding appropriately.
g. Factors in the environment: Communication can also be affected by noise, distractions, and other environmental factors. For instance, it may be challenging to communicate effectively in a noisy or crowded setting.

There are many probable causes of poor communication skills, and it is possible to be impacted by many of them at once. By identifying the underlying causes of their poor communication, people may develop a plan to improve their communication skills and overcome any difficulties they may be running against.

One may enhance their communication skills by using a number of techniques such as:

a. Practice: A person will feel more at ease and confident the more they practice their communication skills. This could mean practicing with friends or family, enrolling in a class on public speaking, or looking for opportunities to speak in front of other people.
b. Continuous listening: Active listening is an essential component of the two-way process of effective communication. Giving the other person your full attention,

asking questions to help you understand, and summarizing what you've heard to make sure you understood it correctly are all part of this process.

c. Understanding communication without speaking: Body language, voice tone, and facial expressions are examples of nonverbal communication that frequently convey more than words alone. Communication can be improved by effectively interpreting and responding to nonverbal cues.
d. Preventing presumptions: Misunderstandings can result from people's presumptions that they know what other people are thinking or feeling. Instead, it's important to ask questions and get answers to make sure you know everything about the situation.
e. To get feedback: It can be helpful to learn from mistakes and identify areas for improvement by soliciting feedback from others.
f. Using language that is clear and concise: Ensure that your message is effectively communicated by using language that is clear, simple, and easy to understand.
g. Identifying and overcoming obstacles: Communication may be hindered by personal or environmental factors, such as noise or social anxiety. Communication abilities can be enhanced by identifying and removing these obstacles.

It is essential to keep in mind that improving communication abilities is a process that requires effort and time. People can improve their ability to communicate effectively in all aspects of life with consistent practice and a willingness to learn and improve.

Sheila has difficulty effectively communicating in both her personal and professional life. Sheila finds it difficult to communicate her feelings and emotions to her friends and family in her personal life. She frequently holds back her opinions and lacks self-confidence, which can result in misunderstandings and disagreements.

Sheila has communication issues in her professional life with coworkers and managers. She frequently struggles to clearly articulate her thoughts and ideas during meetings because she finds it difficult to do so. As a result, chances for professional development and advancement have been missed. Sheila's lack of confidence may be one reason for her difficulty communicating. Sheila may experience anxiety and self-doubt because of her inability to communicate effectively. Sheila may also not have had many opportunities to practice her communication skills, which can cause her to lack confidence and experience.

Sheila's difficulty communicating may also be caused by her inability to recognize nonverbal cues. It's possible that Sheila is unaware of the affects her body language, voice, and facial expressions have on her message. As a result, there may be misunderstandings and confusion in her communication.

Sheila can practice her communication skills and build confidence by taking steps to improve her communication skills. This could mean looking for opportunities to speak in public or attending workshops on communication. Sheila can also improve her active listening skills to clarify misunderstandings and gain a deeper understanding of other people's points of view. Sheila can also work on using language that is both clear and concise, as well as identifying and addressing any barriers to effective communication, such as shyness or anxiety. Sheila can improve her communication abilities and become a more effective communicator in all aspects of her life with consistent effort and practice.

In both personal and professional settings, a lack of communication skills can be a significant obstacle. Building strong relationships, resolving disagreements, and achieving personal and professional objectives all depend on effective communication. A person who lacks communication skills may have trouble speaking up, misinterpret the intentions of others, or miss out on opportunities for growth and advancement.

However, the good news is that with practice and effort, communication skills can be improved. Individuals can overcome their lack of communication skills and become more effective communicators by looking for opportunities to boost their confidence, practice their communication skills, and learn about effective communication strategies. People can increase their success in all aspects of their lives and improve their communication skills with consistent effort and a willingness to learn.

19.Lack of Networking

Lack of networking or networking skills is an individual's inability to establish and maintain a professional network of contacts. Building relationships with people in one's field, expanding one's knowledge and expertise, and discovering new opportunities for personal and professional development all require the ability to network, which is an essential skill. Poor networkers may experience feelings of isolation or disconnection from their industry, miss out on opportunities for career advancement or collaboration, and have difficulty connecting with others in their field. Additionally, they may have difficulty conveying their expertise and value to others, resulting in missed growth and development opportunities.

A lack of social skills, a lack of confidence, a fear of rejection, and a failure to recognize the value of networking are some of the most common causes of poor networking skills. However, individuals can improve their networking abilities and overcome these obstacles with practice and effort.

Attending industry events, participating in online forums, and following up with contacts to maintain those relationships are all necessary for effective networking. Individuals can enhance their networking abilities and personal and professional development by learning efficient networking strategies and actively establishing relationships.

Lack of networking skills in life can be caused by several factors, including:

a. Inadequate awareness: It's possible that some people are unaware of the significance of industry or field-specific networking. It's possible that they don't know how it can help them get ahead in their careers, learn new skills, or take advantage of new opportunities.
b. Inadequate social skills: A lack of social skills may also be the

cause of poor networking skills. In social settings, some people may feel shy or anxious, making it difficult for them to start conversations or form relationships.

c. Aversion to rejection: Another common reason for poor networking skills is a fear of being rejected. People who are afraid of being rejected may avoid networking events or hesitate to contact potential contacts for fear of being ignored.
d. Lack of faith: Networking may also be difficult for those who lack self-esteem or confidence in their abilities. It might be uncomfortable for them to talk about their accomplishments or promote themselves, which makes it difficult for them to form relationships with other people.
e. Chances are limited: Because there aren't many opportunities to network, some people might have trouble. They might work in a field with few opportunities for networking, live in a remote area, or have a small social circle.

It is essential to keep in mind that, with practice and effort, a lack of networking skills can frequently be overcome. People can improve their networking skills and build a strong network of contacts in their industry or field by working to improve their social skills, boosting their confidence, and looking for opportunities to network.

Some options for improving one's ability to network include:

a. Attend events for networking: A great way to meet new people and expand your professional network is to attend networking events. Attend events that are relevant to your profession or industry on a regular basis.
b. Contact coworkers: Request a coffee or lunch meeting with colleagues you admire or respect to discuss industry trends or news. This can help you form relationships and expose you to more of your field's facets.

c. Join associations or groups in your field: You can connect with
colleagues who share your interests and meet new people in your field by joining professional organizations or industry groups.
d. Utilize the internet: LinkedIn and Twitter are two examples of social media platforms that can be useful for expanding your professional network. Make it a point to converse with others in your field or profession and impart your own wisdom.
e. Enhance your communication abilities: The key to successful networking is effective communication. Improve your communication abilities by practicing active listening, asking questions, and making a good impression.
f. Work with other people: Find opportunities to work with others in your field on projects or initiatives together. This could be a great way to meet new people and show off your skills and knowledge.
g. Look for opportunities to mentor others: Having a mentor can be a useful way to learn from someone who has more experience in your field and offer advice. Be proactive in reaching out to potential mentors who you admire and respect to seek their guidance.
h. Be sincere: Keep in mind that building genuine relationships with other people is the goal of networking. Be who you are, be open and honest, and show genuine interest in the work of others.

It may take some time and effort to develop stronger networking abilities, but with some concentration and dedication, you may create a strong professional network that will support your career objectives.

A person's personal and professional life can be significantly impacted by a lack of networking skills, which can result in missed opportunities for career advancement, business expansion, and even personal relationships. Let's look at an example of Natasha, who has difficulty networking:

Natasha has been employed by a company for several years and is prepared for advancement. However, despite her excellent performance and hard work, she has not been promoted. She realizes that this is because she doesn't know how to network. She is shy, so it is hard for her to approach her coworkers, go to networking events, or start a conversation with strangers. Natasha also experiences anxiety whenever she is required to give a public speech or a presentation, which further restricts her capacity for networking and forming relationships. Natasha is frustrated that her talent and hard work are not being recognized because of this, and she also feels stuck in her position. She realizes that she must improve her networking abilities if she wants to advance in her career. Natasha decides to start small by forming relationships with her current coworkers to accomplish this. To get to know her coworkers better, she starts by contacting them and inviting them to lunch or coffee. She also discusses her future objectives and requests feedback on her work.

Natasha also tries to go to company events and volunteer on committees, both of which are opportunities for her to meet new people and develop relationships. She takes classes and joins a local Toastmasters club to practice her public speaking skills. Natasha gets more used to networking and forming relationships over time. Her efforts bear fruit, and she begins to rise in the company's ranks. She is thrilled to finally be acknowledged for her efforts and abilities when she receives an offer for a higher position.

In conclusion, a person's personal and professional life can be hindered by a lack of networking skills. However, it is possible to improve these skills and develop valuable relationships that can lead to exciting opportunities with practice and effort.

A person's opportunities and professional development may be hampered if they lack the ability to network. In many fields and industries, being able to connect with people and build relationships is important because it can lead to career advancement and other

benefits. It can take time and effort to learn how to network, but it's important to understand how important it is to make and keep professional connections.
Attending networking events, being active on professional social media platforms, contacting potential mentors or industry peers, and looking for opportunities to collaborate on projects or initiatives with others in the same field are all potential ways to improve one's networking skills. Being open to new experiences and actively seeking out opportunities to broaden one's professional network are also essential.

In conclusion, a lack of networking skills can have a negative impact on a person's career and growth opportunities, but it is possible to improve in this area and benefit from a strong professional network with effort and focus.

20.Lack of Leadership

Lack of leadership is the inability to effectively inspire and motivate others to achieve a common goal. The ability to effectively communicate, guide and motivate others, make difficult decisions, solve problems, and inspire trust and confidence in others are all aspects of leadership skills. An individual's personal and professional life can be impacted by a lack of leadership skills, which can limit their capacity to advance in their career, achieve their goals, and build successful relationships with others.

Success in many areas of life, including personal relationships, business, education, and community involvement, depends on having leadership qualities. A person's inability to effectively communicate, make sound decisions, resolve conflicts, and inspire others can be hindered by a lack of these skills. Low productivity, a lack of motivation, and a failure to achieve goals and objectives are all possible outcomes of this.

Training, education, and hands-on experience are all ways to improve one's leadership abilities. It is essential for individuals to concentrate on improving their listening, problem-solving, and communication abilities. Additionally, they should work on improving their emotional intelligence, which is the capacity to comprehend and control one's own emotions in addition to those of others. Individuals can also enhance their leadership abilities by seeking mentorship or direction from more seasoned leaders.

In life, a lack of leadership skills can be caused by several different things. Several possibilities include:

a. Lack of knowledge: Through practice and experience, leadership abilities can be developed. It's possible that a person doesn't have the skills necessary to lead and manage a team effectively if they haven't had a lot of experience leading other people or holding positions of authority.

b. Lack of education: Similarly, it may be difficult for a person to
acquire the skills necessary to be an effective leader if they haven't received adequate leadership skills training.
c. Aversion to failure: People may be reluctant to assume leadership roles or make decisions out of fear of failure. This fear may be brought on by a lack of self-assurance in their abilities, which may in turn lead them to question their capacity for making decisions.
d. Self-awareness deficit: Self-awareness and knowing one's own strengths and weaknesses are essential for effective leadership. Self-awareness can hinder a person's growth as a leader because they may not know where they need to improve.
e. Communication difficulties: Effective communication skills are essential for leaders to have. It may be difficult for someone with poor communication skills to convey their ideas and inspire their team.
f. Vision issues: A leader must have a crystal-clear idea of what they want to accomplish and how they will get there. It may be difficult for a person to inspire and motivate their team if they lack a clear strategy or vision.

A lack of leadership skills could be caused by several different things. For a person to work on improving their skills in those areas, it is essential to identify the specific causes.

A lack of leadership abilities can be dealt with in life in several ways:

a. Obtain coaching and mentorship: Finding a coach or mentor can help you improve your leadership abilities. A coach or mentor can help you develop your leadership skills and give you feedback on your strengths and weaknesses.

b. Participate in development and training programs: Individuals can acquire leadership skills through a variety of training and development options. These can be in-person or online, and they can be short courses or long-term programs.
c. Make use of self-reflection: Individuals can increase their self-awareness and gain a better understanding of how to improve their leadership abilities by taking some time to reflect on their own strengths and areas for growth.
d. Adopt leadership positions: People can improve their leadership abilities by looking for leadership opportunities like volunteering for a leadership position in a community organization or taking on a leadership role at work.
e. Learn from books: On leadership, there are numerous books, articles, and other resources that can assist individuals in improving their leadership abilities. Individuals can develop their own leadership abilities by reading about and learning about various leadership styles and methods.

It's important to remember that learning how to be a leader takes time and effort, so you need to be patient and persistent.

A person's lack of leadership skills can manifest in a variety of ways and come from a variety of sources. Let's take Lucas as an illustration because he struggles with his lack of leadership abilities both personally and professionally. Lucas struggles to exercise authority and make decisions. He prefers to let others take the lead and avoids conflicts. He finds it difficult to delegate work and frequently tries to do everything himself, which causes stress and burnout. Additionally, Lucas struggles to inspire and motivate others and fails to effectively convey his vision and objectives. His team members feel disengaged and unmotivated as a result.

Lucas's lack of leadership abilities could be the result of several factors.
It's possible that he has never held a leadership position before, and he lacks the training and experience necessary to acquire the skills.

Additionally, he may be afraid of failing or making mistakes and lack self-assurance. It's possible that Lucas has also developed a passive or non-confrontational personality, making it challenging for him to take charge and make difficult choices.

Lucas has a few options for dealing with his lack of leadership abilities. He can begin by seeking coaching or training in leadership, both of which can assist him in acquiring the abilities necessary to improve as a leader. He can also practice decision-making and delegation in his personal and professional lives, gradually moving up to more senior leadership positions. Additionally, Lucas can work on improving his communication abilities, such as effective public speaking and active listening, which can assist him in inspiring and motivating the members of his team. Lucas can also work on increasing his self-assurance and developing a more assertive personality, both of which can assist him in taking charge and making decisions when necessary.

In conclusion, leadership abilities are necessary in a variety of settings, both personal and professional. A person's ability to succeed and communicate with others can be significantly impacted by a lack of leadership skills. A lack of confidence, poor communication, and a lack of self-awareness are all potential contributors to a lack of leadership skills. But there are a lot of possible ways to help people deal with their lack of leadership skills, such as getting mentorship or coaching, going to workshops or training, practicing good communication, and actively looking for opportunities to learn how to lead. Individuals can improve their ability to lead and achieve success in a variety of areas of their lives by taking action and actively working to improve their leadership skills.

21.Lack of Creativity

Lack of creativity is a condition in which an individual has difficulty coming up with novel concepts, ideas, or solutions in life. This could show up as a lack of originality, creativity, or innovation, and it could have an impact on work, relationships, and personal development. It can be brought on by several things, such as a lack of inspiration, a fear of failing, and cultural or environmental influences that discourage creative thinking. However, it is essential to keep in mind that everyone possesses some level of creativity, which can be enhanced with practice and effort. People who aren't creative may have trouble coming up with new ways to solve problems, may rely a lot on already-existing ideas or solutions, and may have trouble adapting to new challenges or situations. They might also have trouble coming up with original or creative ideas or ways to express themselves.

However, it is essential to keep in mind that creativity does not come naturally to all people, and that some people are born with it while others do not. Instead, creativity is a skill that can be learned and cultivated over time through deliberate practice, exposure to new experiences and concepts, and a willingness to experiment and take risks.

Life's lack of creativity can be caused by several things, including the following:

a. Aversion to failure: Fear of failure is one of the most common causes of poor creativity. Fear of failure prevents many people from trying new things or taking risks. Because they are afraid of failing, people might be afraid to try new things or take chances. This fear may prevent them from coming up with novel concepts and expressing their creativity.
b. Absence of Motivation: A creative block can also be caused by a lack of inspiration on occasion. It can be difficult for

someone to come up with innovative solutions if they are not exposed to
novel concepts or experiences.

c. Negative self-talk: Creativity can also be stifled by negative self-talk. It may be difficult for someone to realize their creative potential if they constantly criticize themselves or believe they are not creative.
d. Anxiety and stress: A person's creativity can also be harmed by stress and anxiety. Creative thinking may be difficult for someone who is worried or overwhelmed. It may be difficult for people to access their creative side when they are stressed or anxious. It can be hard to think creatively or come up with new ideas when the brain's fight-or-flight response takes over.
e. Lack of drive: A creative block can also be brought on by a lack of motivation. It may be challenging for someone to come up with novel and creative concepts if they do not have a strong passion for the work they are doing.
f. Monotony and routine: A lack of originality can result from doing the same thing repeatedly. The mind can become stuck if there is no change and no chance for growth. It can be difficult for people who are not challenged or who are stuck in a routine to think creatively or come up with new ideas.
g. low self-worth: People who have low self-esteem may not have the self-assurance to try new things and take chances, which can stop them from being creative.
h. Resources are scarce: Creativity may be difficult for those who lack access to the necessary resources, such as time, money, or materials.

A lack of creativity is frequently brought on by several different factors, some of which include these. To effectively address the issue, it is essential to identify the specific cause of one's lack of creativity.

Lack of creativity can be overcome in several ways:

a. Meditation and mindfulness practices: Mindfulness can help you focus on the here and now and get rid of any thoughts that are keeping you from being creative.
b. Get a break: Taking a break from a project or job can sometimes help you see things from a different angle and come up with new ideas.
c. Try a new activity: Breaking out of your routine and trying something new can help you come up with fresh ideas.
d. Work with other people: New ideas and perspectives can be brought to the table by working with other people.
e. Maintain a creative diary: You can keep track of your creative thoughts and use them as inspiration in the future by writing them down in sketches, ideas, or any other form.
f. Make use of brainstorming: Getting your creative juices flowing can be aided by setting aside time to think about and come up with ideas.
g. Find sources of inspiration all around you: Art, music, and books are just a few of the things that will inspire you in your surroundings.

You can help overcome a lack of creativity and develop a more innovative and imaginative mindset by incorporating these practices into your daily routine.

Ragini is a software developer who has been employed by the same business for several years. She performs well at work and has previously been promoted. Ragini, on the other hand, is having trouble coming up with fresh concepts for a team project after her boss recently asked for them. She tries to come up with new strategies during brainstorming sessions, but she keeps coming back to the same old ones. Ragini is worried that her coworkers and boss will perceive her as uncreative or unproductive because she is feeling stuck and lacking in motivation. She is unsure of how to break out of this creative rut and come up with novel project concepts. Ragini can work on improving her creativity in several ways, some of which are as follows:

a. Practicing creativity at work: Her ability to think creatively will improve as she engages in more creative activities. She can engage in any creative endeavor she chooses, including dancing, drawing, writing, and painting.
b. Getting motivated: Books, movies, music, and other creative works can serve as sources of inspiration for her. This may assist her in developing novel project strategies and concepts.
c. Routine deviation: Routine and structure can sometimes stifle creativity. To encourage creativity, Ragini can try breaking out of her routine, doing things in a new or different way, or going beyond her comfort zone.
d. Collaboration: Collaboration with people who have different points of view can help spark creativity. She can join a group of creative people or work with others to come up with new ideas.
e. Relaxation technique: Creativity can be hindered by stress and anxiety. Ragini can try relaxation methods like yoga, meditation, or breathing exercises to help her feel less stressed and more creative.
f. Taking risks: Creativity can be severely hampered by anxiety about failing. Ragini can work on taking chances and not being afraid to make mistakes because doing so can help her come up with fresh concepts and creative breakthroughs.
g. Practicing brainstorming: Spend some time brainstorming as many ideas as you can without criticizing or editing them.
h. Challenging yourself: Challenge yourself by stepping outside of your comfort zone, trying something new, and going beyond
what you think is possible for you.

i. Have an open mind and a curious mind: Investigate new possibilities, ask questions, and approach issues with a readiness to try new things.

People like Ragini can overcome their lack of creativity and create a more innovative and imaginative mentality by using these techniques.

In conclusion, individuals may experience difficulties due to lack of creativity in both personal and professional settings. Several things, including the fear of failing, a lack of inspiration, and ineffective time management, can contribute to it. But there are many ways to boost creativity, including trying new things, working with others, and taking breaks from mundane tasks. It is crucial to understand that creativity is a skill that can be improved over time with effort and practice. People like Ragini can overcome their lack of creativity and realize their full potential by using these tactics, committing to a creative mentality and unlocking their full potential.

22.Lack of Adaptability

Lack of adaptability is an individual's inability to adapt to new situations, changes, or circumstances. This could be in your personal or professional life, and it could mean adjusting to new social situations, interpersonal relationships, or work environments. An inability to accept or embrace new ideas, resistance to change, difficulty making decisions or solving problems, or a general feeling of discomfort or anxiety in unfamiliar situations are all signs of a lack of adaptability. Because change is constant and inevitable in today's world, being adaptable has become increasingly important. People who aren't flexible might have trouble keeping up with new ideas, technologies, and trends, which could hurt their personal and professional development.

In life, a lack of adaptability can be caused by several different things. Some common ones are as follows:

a. Change phobia: When confronted with novel or divergent circumstances, many people exhibit resistance to change and experience anxiety or stress.
b. Lack of experience: It can be difficult for someone to adapt to new circumstances if they haven't been exposed to a variety of experiences, cultures, and settings.
c. Perfectionism: Because they are often rigid in their thinking and have trouble adapting to new circumstances or setbacks, perfectionists may be less adaptable.
d. Self-awareness deficit: Self-aware individuals may not recognize when they are having trouble adapting and may be less likely to seek assistance or make changes.
e. Problems with one's health: A person's ability to adapt to new situations or changes in their environment can be hindered by mental or physical health issues.
f. Dependence too much on routine: When confronted with new or unexpected circumstances, individuals who place a high

value on routine and familiarity may have difficulty adapting.

g. Lack of drive: A person may be less likely to acquire the abilities and mindset necessary to adapt to new situations if they lack a strong desire to learn and develop.

A lack of adaptability in life may be caused by several different factors. It is essential to keep in mind that every individual's circumstance is distinct, and the factors that contribute to a lack of adaptability can vary from person to person.

Life adaptability can be improved in several ways. Some possible solutions are as follows:

a. Accept change: Being open to new experiences and accepting that change is a normal part of life is a great way to become more adaptable.
b. Be adaptable: A certain amount of adaptability is needed to improve one's capacity for adjusting to a variety of circumstances. This means being willing to change your behavior and expectations when necessary.
c. Staying positive: Keeping a positive attitude can help you cope with change and remain resilient and adaptable.
d. Make mindfulness a habit: Meditation and other mindfulness practices can help you stay in the now and improve your ability to adjust to new situations.
e. Find new experiences to try: You can improve your adaptability by trying new things and learning new skills and perspectives.
f. Learning from experiences: You can identify areas in which you could have been more adaptable and develop strategies to improve in the future by reflecting on past experiences.

In general, adaptability can only be developed by being open to change, flexible, and committed to learning and development. Anyone can improve their adaptability and ability to navigate life's ups and downs by practicing these skills.

Life is full of examples of people who are unable to change.

A lack of adaptability can manifest itself in a variety of ways for Ravi. When confronted with new or different circumstances, Ravi may, for instance, be unwilling to compromise or adjust a set of rules or beliefs.

Ravi may not be able to adjust to the changing environment and take advantage of new opportunities as a result, which can prevent him from achieving his goals.

Additionally, relationships can be difficult to form if one lacks adaptability. It's possible that Ravi will not be able to adapt to the wants and needs of other people or comprehend their point of view. As a result, Ravi, and the people around him may develop strained relationships as well as a lack of trust and comprehension.

Lastly, Ravi may not be able to adapt to the requirements of a changing environment, which can result in a sense of stagnation. Ravi may believe he is incapable of making positive changes in his life as a result, which can result in a lack of motivation.

Ravi 's life can suffer greatly from a lack of adaptability, which can also limit his chances of happiness and success. Therefore, it is essential for Ravi to work on improving his capacity for adaptability and being open to novel concepts and circumstances.

23.Lack of Innovation

Lack of innovation is a situation in which a person or organization fails to come up with novel and creative ideas or solutions to problems. Creativity, innovative thinking, and the discovery of novel and improved methods are all essential components of innovation. People who lack innovation may have difficulty coming up with novel concepts or adapting to changes in their surroundings. This can result in a lack of progress, missed opportunities, and stagnation. Business, science, technology, and the arts are just a few of the many fields in which innovation plays an important role. Progress can be sluggish or nonexistent without innovation. People who aren't innovative might find it hard to keep up with changes in their industry, fail to come up with exciting new products or services, or miss out on opportunities to make their own or other people's lives better.

Innovation can be challenging because it necessitates taking chances, being open to novel concepts, and being willing to experiment. It's not always easy to come up with creative solutions to problems, but there are a lot of ways to encourage creativity and innovation. Collaboration, experimentation, and ongoing learning and development are all examples of these.

Life's lack of creativity can be caused by a variety of factors, including:

a. Aversion to failure: People who are afraid of failing are less likely to try new things, take chances, or think outside the box, which can make it harder for them to come up with creative ideas.
b. Acceptance of the status quo: Some people may get too used to their routine or way of doing things, which can make them resistant to change and make them less likely to try new things.

c. Inadequate exposure to diverse perspectives: It's possible that a person won't be exposed to novel concepts or ways of thinking if they only hang out with people who share their perspectives and experiences.
d. Scarcity of Resources: A person's ability to innovate can also be hampered by a lack of resources like time, money, or access to information.
e. A lack of drive: It may be difficult for someone to innovate if they lack the drive or motivation to think creatively and generate novel concepts.
f. Lack of skills or knowledge: It may be difficult for someone to come up with new ideas if they lack the knowledge or skills necessary for innovation, such as technical or problem-solving skills.
g. Lack of assistance: It can also be difficult for someone to innovate and take risks if they don't have support from others, such as friends, family, or colleagues.

It is essential to keep in mind that some of these factors may be connected to one another and may build upon one another. For instance, a lack of resources can result in a lack of motivation, which in turn can result in a lack of exposure to various points of view.

The following are some options for dealing with life's lack of innovation:

a. Adopt a "growth mindset": The belief that hard work and dedication can help you improve your intelligence and abilities is known as a growth mindset. You open yourself up to new experiences and are more willing to take risks when you have a growth mindset. This can help you to develop creativity and come up with innovative solutions.
b. Keep an open mind: Innovation can be fueled by curiosity, which is a powerful motivator. It enables you to inquire, seek

out new data, and generate fresh concepts. You can seek out new experiences, investigate new subjects, and ask questions to cultivate curiosity.

c. Work with other people: Innovation is primarily fueled by collaboration. You can develop new perspectives and concepts that will enable you to be more creative by working with people who have different experiences and points of view.
d. Try new things and take chances: Trying new things and taking risks are two common aspects of innovation. You can learn what works and what doesn't by trying out new ideas and coming up with new solutions to old problems.
e. Stay up to date: Being aware of the most recent developments and trends in your field can help you become more creative. Attending conferences, reading industry publications, and networking with others in your field are all examples of this.
f. Engage in creative activities: Exercises in creativity can help you think creatively and come up with new ideas. Free writing, mind mapping, and brainstorming are all examples of creative exercises.

You can begin to improve your ability to innovate and become more creative in both your personal and professional lives by putting these strategies into practice.

Let's consider Ranjan's lack of adaptability throughout his life.

An individual's inability to adapt to shifting circumstances or situations is referred to as "lack of adaptability." Ranjan may have difficulty adjusting to new circumstances or changes in his surroundings. He might have trouble adapting to sudden shifts and prefer to stick to his routine or the familiar. This could be because he is afraid of the unknown, doesn't feel confident, or doesn't want to get out of his comfort zone.

Ranjan, for instance, might have trouble adjusting to a new job with a different set of responsibilities and expectations than his previous one. He may have difficulty adapting to new procedures or working with a new team, which may result in lower levels of productivity and job satisfaction.

It is essential to keep in mind that a lack of adaptability can affect more than just work. For instance, Ranjan might have a hard time adjusting to changes in his personal life, like starting a new relationship or moving to a different city.

Ranjan may need to work on developing certain skills like adaptability, resilience, and openness to change in order to improve his adaptability. He might also benefit from trying new things, pushing himself to get out of his comfort zone, and practicing mindfulness to stay in the now. The underlying issues that may be causing his inability to adapt can also be addressed by seeking support from friends, family, or a therapist.

For personal and professional development, as well as for the advancement of society, innovation is essential. Fear of failure, a lack of resources or skills, and resistance to change are all potential causes of a lack of innovation.

It is essential to cultivate a growth mindset, view failure as a learning opportunity, and constantly seek out new experiences and challenges to overcome a lack of innovation. Various activities, such as brainstorming, experimenting, and working with others, can also help one develop their creativity. Additionally, new ideas and approaches can be sparked by seeking out and learning from diverse experiences and new perspectives.

Overall, individuals can overcome a lack of innovation and achieve personal and professional growth by adopting innovation as a core value and continually looking for new ways to develop and implement innovative ideas.

24.Lack of Strategic Thinking

Lack of strategic thinking in life is the inability to think and plan strategically in various aspects of life. It indicates that a person is unable to identify and evaluate the information that is available, to plan, and to make decisions based on long-term objectives and goals. A lack of purpose and direction missed opportunities, and even failure to achieve desired outcomes are all possible outcomes of this. The ability to assess and evaluate situations, identify potential challenges and opportunities, and develop a long-term strategy that is in line with the overall goals and objectives are all components of strategic thinking. It requires creative thinking and the ability to anticipate potential roadblocks that could impede progress.

In life, there are several things that can lead to a lack of strategic thinking. Common reasons include:

a. A lack of experience: A person's capacity for strategic thinking can be hampered if they are not exposed to a variety of situations. A person may lack the experience necessary to make informed decisions if they have not been exposed to a variety of situations.
b. Specific focus: It's possible that people who have a narrow focus on a few areas won't be able to see the bigger picture or how different situations are connected to one another. They may be unable to think strategically because of this.
c. Lack of interest: Because it encourages people to inquire and find information, curiosity is essential for strategic thinking. A person may not be motivated to gather the information they need to think strategically if they lack curiosity.
d. Aversion to failure: Risk-taking and decision-making that require strategic thinking can be thwarted by fear. A person may choose to make decisions based on short-term goals rather than long-term objectives because of this.

e. Lack of structure: A person's inability to think strategically can be hindered by a lack of structure in their life. Focusing on long-term objectives and making decisions that are in line with those objectives can be challenging in the absence of a routine or plan.
f. A narrow perspective: Individuals with narrow perspectives might not be able to understand how their actions affect other people or the greater system. This can lead them to take non-strategic decisions.

Several factors might contribute to a lack of strategic thinking in daily living. These are only a handful of the numerous factors that might contribute to a person's lack of strategic thinking.

To address the problem of poor strategic thinking, some possible solutions include:

a. Enhance your skills and knowledge: Enhancing your skills and knowledge is the first step in developing strategic thinking. You can attend training programs, read books, and look for mentorship from experts in your field. In addition to exposing, you to new ways of thinking and problem-solving, this can assist you in acquiring fresh perspectives and concepts.
b. Evaluate and analyze: To find the opportunities and challenges in your situation, it's critical to evaluate and analyze it. Consider the bigger picture while taking a break from your day-to-day activities. What are the prevailing trends in your sector? What are your rivals up to? What are your organization's advantages and disadvantages? By responding to these questions, you can learn more about the areas in which you need to focus your attention and how to overcome obstacles.

c. Create a strategy: You need to come up with a strategy to deal with the problems and take advantage of the opportunities once you have assessed and assessed your situation. Your assessment of the circumstance and your expertise ought to serve as the foundation for this strategy. It ought to be understandable, brief, and clear.
d. Make a move: If you don't act, even the best plan is pointless. You must put your plan into action after developing it. Discipline, perseverance, and the capacity to change with the times are all necessary for this.
e. Obtain input and adapt: It's critical to seek input on your strategy and make the appropriate adjustments. You can ask coworkers, mentors, and other stakeholders for their opinions. By doing so, you may find any holes or weak points in your strategy and make the required changes to assist you reach your objectives.

These actions will help you improve your strategic thinking abilities and increase your effectiveness in reaching your objectives.

The process of evaluating a situation, collecting and evaluating information, and then deciding how to proceed based on that information is known as strategic thinking. It is a crucial component of decision-making, planning, and problem-solving. Priya may face a variety of challenges as a result of her lack of strategic thinking.

Priya may struggle to make decisions that are in her best interest if she does not have strategic thinking skills. She might become easily overwhelmed by the options and have trouble picking a course of action. Additionally, she may be more likely to act impulsively and disregard long-term consequences.

Priya may also have trouble making plans and setting goals if she lacks strategic thinking. She might end up in a cycle of day-to-day survival if she doesn't have a plan, never taking the time to think about the bigger picture and how she can use her skills and resources to reach her long-term objectives.

Priya's inability to think strategically can also make it easy for her to become easily frustrated with the challenges she faces in life. She might get stuck and not be able to move forward if she doesn't take the time to look at the situation and come up with creative solutions.

In the end, Priya won't be able to make the most of her life and reach her full potential if she doesn't think strategically. She needs to put in the time to learn this skill if she wants to make better decisions, set and achieve goals, and live a more satisfying life.

Finally, we must comprehend that a lack of strategic thinking results in a lack of direction, purpose, and concentration in life. It is challenging to plan and carry out goals in a meaningful and successful manner without strategic thinking. It can also result in lost chances and a lack of innovation. Additionally, it may result in a loss of motivation and a sensation of overload. In general, strategic thinking is an essential component of success and need to be prioritized in daily life.

25.Lack of Technology Skills

Lack of technology skills is a person's inability to use technology effectively. This could include a wide range of abilities, like how to use a computer, the internet, social media, and other digital tools. It has become increasingly important for people to develop these skills to succeed in both personal and professional settings as technology have become more integrated into our daily lives. A person's ability to complete certain tasks, communicate effectively, and keep up with the pace of technology in today's world can be hindered by a lack of technological skills. A person who has trouble using basic word processing software or email, for instance, may have trouble keeping up with their job responsibilities. Also, if you don't know how to use social media, you might miss out on opportunities to network or have trouble keeping in touch with friends and family who use these platforms.

Individuals' lack of technology skills can be caused by a variety of factors, but the following are some common ones:

a. Inaccessibility to technology: It can be difficult for someone to learn and improve their technology skills if they do not have access to technology, such as a smartphone or computer.
b. Aversion to technology: Technology may intimidate some individuals or cause them to be afraid that they will damage something if they try to use it.
c. Absence of interest: It's possible that some people simply lack an interest in technology and do not try to learn.
d. Method of study: Different people learn in different ways, and some people may have trouble with technology if they don't have access to the right resources or teaching methods that work for them.
e. Age: It may be harder for older adults to acquire new technology skills because they did not grow up with the internet or other modern technology.

f. linguistic obstacles: It may be challenging to comprehend how to utilize technology for those who speak a language other than the one that technology resources are typically available in.

A lack of technology skills can occur for several reasons, some of which are listed above.

There are a few things you can do to improve your life if you struggle with a lack of technology skills:

a. Identifying the specific technological abilities, you need to improve: Find out which technological abilities are necessary for your job, personal interests, or other requirements. You might need to learn more advanced skills like coding, data analysis, or web development, or you might need to learn more fundamental computer applications like word processing, spreadsheets, or presentation software.
b. Look for training opportunities: Find online tutorials, workshops, or training courses that can help you learn the skills you need. Community colleges, online courses, and coding bootcamps are just a few of the many options for technology education.
c. Practicing on regular basis: Practice frequently to consolidate your knowledge and abilities after determining the skills you need to improve and locating appropriate training resources. Work on your own projects or exercises, or take on freelance work, to improve your skills and gain practical experience.
d. Look for peers or mentors: Seek guidance from people who are experts in the skills you want to develop. You can meet people who share your interests by joining online communities or meetups.

e. Keep up with the latest technology trends: So that you can remain relevant and up to date on the most recent developments, keep an eye on technology trends and industry shifts.
f. Be persistent and patient: Be patient and persistent in your efforts to improve your technology skills because it takes time and effort to do so. To keep yourself motivated and focused on your growth, set attainable goals, and monitor your progress over time.

You can overcome a lack of technology skills and improve your ability to navigate the modern digital world by following the above steps.

There are several factors that can be attributed to Neil's lack of technological skills in life. As a child or young adult, Neil may not have had access to technology, or he may not have been given the opportunity to learn how to use technology. It's possible that he was resistant to learning new technologies or that he struggled to comprehend technology's concepts and functions.

Technology is a necessary component of modern life, and success necessitates the ability to use it effectively. The opportunities Neil has to learn, work, and remain competitive may be limited by his lack of technology skills. He may also be unable to access resources and services or communicate effectively with others as a result.

Neil should start by familiarizing himself with fundamental ideas like how to use a computer and the internet to improve his technology skills. He should also think about enrolling in classes or courses to learn more about technology and how to use it well. Lastly, to assist him in comprehending and utilizing technology, he ought to make use of online tutorials, resources, and support networks. Neil can become more at ease with technology and better prepared to take advantage of its opportunities with enough practice and direction.

26.Lack of Emotional Intelligence

Lack of emotional intelligence is the inability to recognize and control one's own emotions as well as those of others, resulting in poor interpersonal relationships and communication. The ability to perceive and comprehend emotions, use emotions to direct thought and behavior, and manage and regulate emotions in oneself and others are all components of emotional intelligence. It can be difficult for people with low emotional intelligence to comprehend or appropriately express their own emotions, which can make it difficult for them to form relationships and make decisions. Additionally, they may have difficulty interpreting other people's feelings, resulting in misunderstandings and arguments. This can make it hard to build and keep healthy relationships, both at work and in your personal life.

Lack of emotional intelligence in life can be caused by a variety of factors. Several possibilities include:

a. Inadequate awareness: Emotional intelligence can be hard to develop in some people because they may not understand how others feel or how they feel.
b. Negative role models: It may be difficult for a person to acquire these abilities if they were surrounded by people who did not place a high value on emotional intelligence or did not grow up with positive role models.
c. Trauma: A person's capacity to control their own emotions or comprehending the emotions of others can be affected by experiencing emotional distress or trauma.
d. Character traits: Some people may have personality traits that make it hard for them to connect emotionally with other people or control their own emotions.
e. Lack of practice: Emotional intelligence, like any other skill, needs practice to get better. It may be difficult for a person to develop these skills if they have not had many opportunities to practice emotional intelligence.

It is essential to keep in mind that lack of emotional intelligence can be brought on by a variety of different factors, and that no two people's experiences are the same.

Emotional intelligence can be developed in a variety of ways:

a. Make self-awareness a habit: Begin by recognizing your own biases, emotions, and triggers. You will be able to better comprehend how you react emotionally to various situations because of this.
b. Enhance empathy: Put yourself in the shoes of other people and try to comprehend their feelings and points of view. You might find that this helps you connect with other people and communicate with them better.
c. Engage in active listening by: Continuously and attentively pay attention to what others are saying and respond thoughtfully.
d. Practicing self-control: Learn to control your own feelings, impulses, and reactions to various circumstances. Mindfulness, meditation, and relaxation exercises are all examples of this.
e. Learn how to communicate effectively: Improve your nonverbal communication, conflict resolution, and assertiveness in communication skills.
f. Obtain feedback: Be open to constructive criticism and suggestions for improvement, as well as asking for feedback on
your emotional intelligence skills from others.
g. Get professional assistance: A good first step in developing emotional intelligence is to seek professional assistance from a therapist or counselor if you are experiencing significant emotional difficulties or difficulties in your relationships.

Let's talk more about what it means for a person named Rana to lack emotional intelligence in their life.

The ability to recognize, comprehend, and control one's own emotions, as well as to perceive, interpret, and respond appropriately to the emotions of others, is referred to as emotional intelligence (EI). Therefore, a deficiency in these areas is referred to as a lack of emotional intelligence, and it can result in a variety of negative outcomes in both personal and professional life.

A lack of emotional intelligence can manifest itself in a variety of ways for Rana, including:

a. Difficulty managing emotions: Rana may have difficulty maintaining emotional control and be prone to sudden outbursts of rage or frustration.
b. Insensitivity to other people's feelings: Rana may have trouble understanding or responding to other people's emotions, which can lead to misunderstandings or conflict.
c. Communication difficulties: In emotionally charged situations, Rana may struggle to communicate effectively with others, resulting in misunderstandings or ineffective communication.
d. Inability to establish and maintain relationships: Due to a lack of emotional awareness and appropriate emotional responses, Rana may have difficulty establishing and maintaining positive relationships with others.
e. Inability to deal with stress: Rana may have difficulty managing stress, which could result in increased anxiety, burnout, or other undesirable outcomes.

Rana may consider several options to address a lack of emotional intelligence, such as:

a. Getting professional assistance: Rana might gain from seeking the guidance and support of a therapist, counselor, or coach who specializes in emotional intelligence.
b. Acquiring self-awareness skills: Rana might gain from learning how to better manage their own emotions and becoming more aware of their own feelings.
c. Increasing empathy: Empathy training, which entails putting oneself in the position of another person and comprehending their feelings and points of view, may be beneficial for Rana.
d. Enhancing communication abilities: To avoid misunderstandings and improve relationships, Rana may benefit from improving their communication skills, particularly in emotionally charged situations.
e. Taking part in activities that reduce stress: To better cope with stress, Rana may benefit from participating in activities that reduce stress, like meditation, exercise, or other forms of self-care.

In general, addressing a lack of emotional intelligence necessitates self-reflection, developing new abilities, and seeking professional guidance and support as required.

An individual's personal and professional life can be negatively impacted by a lack of emotional intelligence because it can make it difficult to comprehend and manage one's own emotions as well as those of others. The good news, though, is that emotional intelligence is a skill that can be learned and honed over time with the right methods and tools.

Self-awareness, or the capacity to recognize and comprehend one's own emotions and how they influence one's thoughts and actions, is one key to enhancing emotional intelligence. This might necessitate pondering one's own emotional responses to various circumstances and how they might be perceived by others. Empathy, or the capacity to comprehend and connect with the emotions of others, is yet another crucial component of emotional intelligence. This might entail paying close attention to what other people are saying, considering their point of view, and acknowledging the feelings they are expressing.

A person's ability to communicate effectively can assist them in expressing their feelings in a healthy and constructive manner and in comprehending the feelings of others. Active listening, using "I" statements to express one's needs and feelings, and practicing effective conflict-resolution strategies are all examples of this.

In conclusion, self-awareness, empathy, and effective communication skills can be developed to address emotional intelligence deficiencies. People can improve their emotional intelligence and reap the benefits in both their personal and professional lives with practice and dedication.

27.Lack of Resilience

Lack of resilience is the inability to deal with and recover from difficult circumstances, setbacks and failures in life. It's the inability to deal with stress and adversity and adapt to change. The capacity to recover and move on from challenging circumstances is a component of resilience. Because it helps people deal with difficult situations, cope with stress and anxiety, and bounce back from setbacks, resilience is an important life trait. However, when confronted with difficulties or setbacks, individuals who lack resilience may experience feelings of overwhelm, anxiety, and lack of motivation. This can result in negative emotions, thoughts, and actions that have a negative impact on a person's relationships, career, and personal growth.

Lack of resilience in life can be caused by a variety of factors, some of which include:

a. Insufficient social support: A lack of social support, such as that provided by friends or family, can make it challenging to deal with challenging circumstances and may reduce resilience.
b. Patterns of negative thinking: Negative thinking styles like pessimism, overgeneralization, and catastrophizing can make it harder to deal with challenges, which can lower resilience.
c. Trauma: Abuse or a natural disaster, for example, can have a long-lasting effect on a person's ability to overcome challenges.
d. Constant stress: A person's ability to deal with adversity and resilience can be weakened by chronic stress.
e. Inability to manage stress: People who don't have good coping skills, like how to solve problems and deal with stress, may find it harder to deal with difficult situations and may be less resilient as a result.

f. Self-care neglect: Poor self-care, like not getting enough sleep, not exercising, or not eating well, can make it harder to deal with stress and make it harder to be resilient.
g. Scarcity of Positive experiences: By reducing positive emotions and social support, a lack of positive experiences, such as meaningful relationships or hobbies, can make it harder to build resilience.

A lack of resilience can be brought on by many different things. Recognizing that resilience is a complex and multifaceted quality, and that different people may struggle with it for a variety of reasons is essential.

There are a few things you can do to improve your resilience and cope with stress and adversity more effectively if you are dealing with a lack of resilience in your life. The following are some possible strategies for dealing with resilience deficits:

a. Create a positive attitude: Reframe negative thoughts so that they focus on the positive. Create a sense of hope and optimism.
b. Relaxation and mindfulness practices should be practiced: Yoga, mindfulness meditation, and other methods of relaxation can help you relax, clear your mind, and focus more clearly.
c. Establish a support system: Develop a support network and keep in touch with your friends, family, and other loved ones. This can assist you in coping with stress and adversity and serve as a source of emotional support.
d. Make time for yourself: Eat well, exercise regularly, and get enough sleep to take care of your physical and emotional health.
e. Take away what you've learned: Consider your setbacks and

failures as learning opportunities. Make the most of your experiences to improve your resilience and problem-solving abilities.

f. Get professional assistance: Consider consulting a mental health professional for guidance and support if you are having trouble developing your resilience on your own.

Keep in mind that it takes time, effort, and patience to build resilience. You can, however, gradually increase your resilience and become better prepared to face life's challenges by starting with small steps and focusing on the good things in your life.

The term "lack of resilience" refers to an individual's inability to recover from difficult or challenging circumstances. This could indicate that Sofia struggles to overcome obstacles and adapt to change. An illustration of how this might manifest in her life is as follows:

Sofia has always done well in school, earning top grades and getting involved in extracurricular activities. However, once she enrolls in college, she encounters difficulties balancing her part-time job, social life, and coursework. She feels overwhelmed and discouraged because she misses a few assignments, which lowers her grades. She becomes paralyzed and begins to skip classes and neglect her responsibilities instead of seeking assistance or changing her approach. As a result, her academic performance suffers as she struggles to catch up and continues to fall further behind.

In this case, Sofia is unable to adapt to the new challenges she faces in college because she lacks resilience. She is unable to bounce back from setbacks because she allows them to overwhelm her.

Sofia may need to work on developing coping mechanisms, establishing a support network, and changing her mindset in order to improve her resilience. This may entail seeking support from friends, family, or a therapist, practicing self-care, setting attainable goals, and cultivating a growth mindset that places an emphasis on overcoming obstacles and learning from them rather than giving up. Sofia can better adapt to life's challenges and acquire the self-assurance and abilities she needs to succeed by developing resilience.

People who lack resilience may face significant obstacles in life that prevent them from achieving their objectives and living lives that are full of fulfillment. However, it is essential to keep in mind that resilience is a skill that can be improved over time.

Developing a strong support network, practicing mindfulness and self-care, setting attainable goals, and developing a growth mindset are just a few of the many practices and strategies that can assist individuals in enhancing their resilience. In addition, working through issues related to resilience and developing a more upbeat and proactive outlook can be accomplished by seeking assistance from a therapist or other mental health professional.

Recognizing that developing resilience is a journey that may require time and effort to overcome obstacles and acquire the skills necessary to thrive in the face of adversity is essential. However, it is possible to cultivate greater resilience and lead a life that is more satisfying and fulfilling if you are willing to learn and grow with perseverance, self-awareness, and a willingness to learn.

28.Lack of Stress Management

Lack of stress management is the failure to adequately deal with and manage stress in daily life. Stress is a normal reaction to tough or dangerous circumstances, but when it persists or is too great, it can have negative effects on one's physical and mental health as well as making it harder to carry out everyday chores and obligations. Lack of stress management abilities can make stress worse and have unfavorable effects. Stress is a typical piece of life, and everybody encounters it somewhat, yet when it becomes constant or overpowering, it can adversely affect an individual's physical and emotional well-being, connections, and general prosperity. Lack of stress management skills may make it difficult to deal with life's challenges and can lead to several negative outcomes, including tension, discouragement, burnout, and real physical issues.

There are a few expected reasons for an absence of stress among the executives throughout everyday life. A few normal causes might include:

a. Unfortunate survival techniques: Individuals who need powerful strategies for dealing with especially difficult times might battle to oversee pressure, prompting more noteworthy degrees of tension and pain.
b. Exhaust: Individuals who work extended periods, take on such many liabilities, or have too little free time might find it challenging to deal with their feelings of anxiety.
c. Absence of social help: Individuals who need social help or feel confined may battle to oversee pressure successfully, as they might not have the help, they need to adapt to testing circumstances.
d. Medical issues: Certain ailments or persistent agony can cause pressure and make it hard to oversee pressure.
e. Monetary challenges: Individuals who are battling with monetary troubles might encounter elevated degrees of stress

because of monetary concerns and vulnerability.

f. Injury: Individuals who have encountered horrendous mishaps or continuous injury might find it challenging to deal with their feelings of anxiety.

These are only a few potential causes for low levels of stress across the board in daily life; other factors may also be at play, depending on the circumstances of everyone.

There are numerous successful techniques that can assist an individual with managing an absence of stress on the board throughout everyday life. The following are a couple of likely answers to consider:

a. Recognize the wellspring of stress: The most vital phase in overseeing pressure is to distinguish the wellspring of stress in your life. This could be anything from business-related pressure to relationship issues. When you distinguish the wellspring of stress, you can do whatever it takes to oversee it.
b. Practice unwinding strategies: Unwinding methods like profound breathing, reflection, and yoga can assist you with diminishing feelings of anxiety and advancing serenity.
c. Work out consistently: Exercise is an incredible method for overseeing pressure, as it assists discharge of endorphins that with canning work on your temperament and diminish feelings of anxiety.
d. Get sufficient rest: Getting sufficient rest is significant for general well-being and prosperity and can assist you with better-overseeing pressure.
e. Practice using time effectively: Unfortunately using time effectively can be a significant wellspring of stress. Figuring out how to focus on assignments and deal with your time really can assist with lessening feelings of anxiety.

f. Look for help: On the off chance that you are attempting to oversee weight all alone, think about looking for help from companions, family, or psychological wellness proficient.
g. Consider way-of-life changes: Making sound way of life changes, like decreasing caffeine and liquor utilization, can likewise assist you with better overseeing pressure.

Recall what is happening is special, and what works for one individual may not work for another. It might take experimentation to find the systems that turn out best for you. The significant thing is to make a move and effectively work to oversee pressure in your life.

There are numerous successful techniques that can assist an individual with managing an absence of stress on the board throughout everyday life. The following are a couple of likely answers to consider:

a. Recognize the wellspring of stress: The most vital phase in overseeing pressure is to distinguish the wellspring of stress in your life. This could be anything from business-related pressure to relationship issues. When you distinguish the wellspring of stress, you can do whatever it takes to oversee it.
b. Practice unwinding strategies: Unwinding methods like profound breathing, reflection, and yoga can assist you with diminishing feelings of anxiety and advancing serenity.
c. Work out consistently: Exercise is an incredible method for overseeing pressure, as it assists discharge of endorphins that with canning work on your temperament and diminish feelings of anxiety.
d. Get sufficient rest: Getting sufficient rest is significant for general well-being and prosperity and can assist you with better-overseeing pressure.
e. Practice using time effectively: Unfortunately using time effectively can be a significant wellspring of stress. Figuring

out how to focus on assignments and deal with your time really can assist with lessening feelings of anxiety.

f. Look for help: On the off chance that you are attempting to oversee weight all alone, think about looking for help from companions, family, or psychological wellness proficient.
g. Consider way-of-life changes: Making sound way of life changes, like decreasing caffeine and liquor utilization, can likewise assist you with better overseeing pressure.

Recall what is happening is special, and what works for one individual may not work for another. It might take experimentation to find the systems that turn out best for you. The significant thing is to make a move and effectively work to oversee pressure in your life.

Let's talk more about how a person named Sofia doesn't know how to manage stress in her life.

Sofia is a professional who works hard and has a lot on her plate. She also has two young children and a demanding job that she does full-time. Despite her best efforts, she frequently experiences feelings of stress and overwhelm. Sofia's quality of life, work performance, and interpersonal relationships are all being negatively impacted by her inability to effectively manage her stress levels.

There could be several reasons why Sofia does not know how to control her stress. Among the possibilities are:

a. Ineffective time management skills: It's possible that Sofia isn't effectively managing her time, which can make her feel rushed and stressed. It's possible that she's taking on too much and won't have enough time to complete her tasks and fulfill her responsibilities.
b. Lack of assistance: It's possible that Sofia lacks the support she requires to effectively manage her stress. It might be hard for her to control her stress levels because she might feel alone, overwhelmed, and without support.

c. Patterns of negative thought: It's possible that Sofia has negative thought patterns that make her feel stressed out. She may have a propensity to imagine bad things happening or to focus on the bad, which can make her stressed out even more.
d. Abuse of self-care: It's possible that Sofia isn't taking care of herself physically, mentally, or emotionally. This can make it difficult to effectively manage stress because it can result in feelings of exhaustion and burnout.

Sofia can take several steps to address her lack of stress management skills. Some alternatives include:

a. Management of time: Sofia can work on improving her ability to manage her time effectively. She can organize her projects into smaller, more manageable tasks, establish attainable objectives, and set priorities for them.
b. Seek assistance: Sofia can seek support from others by contacting friends and family, consulting a therapist, or joining a support group.
c. Behavioral and cognitive therapy: Sofia may be able to learn to identify her negative thought patterns and develop more positive and adaptable mental habits through this kind of therapy.
d. Self-care: Sofia has options for enhancing her mental, emotional, and physical health. Exercise, meditation, journaling, and other self-care practices are all examples of this.

Sofia can improve her stress management abilities by following these steps, which may result in a life that is more satisfying and fulfilling. A person's physical, mental, and emotional well-being can be seriously harmed if they don't learn how to manage stress. Anxiety, depression, high blood pressure, heart disease, and other health issues can all result from chronic stress.

It is essential for people to recognize when they are feeling stressed and to take preventative measures to manage it. Developing healthy coping mechanisms for dealing with stressors, seeking support from friends or a mental health professional, and engaging in mindfulness practices like meditation or deep breathing are all examples of this.

It is possible to boost productivity and resilience in the face of difficulties by incorporating stress management strategies into one's daily routine. Starting to prioritize stress management is never too late, and even small steps can have a significant impact on one's life.

29.Lack of Conflict Management

Lack of conflict management is the inability to manage conflicts or disagreements that arise in personal and professional relationships. Communication, negotiation, problem-solving, and emotional regulation are just a few of the skills and behaviors that are required to successfully resolve conflicts. A person who lacks skills in conflict management may find it difficult to resolve disagreements in a way that benefits everyone involved. This can result in ongoing disputes, strained relationships, and negative outcomes in a variety of areas of life.

It's important to remember that conflict is a part of life and can happen in any situation where two or more people have different needs, ideas, or points of view. Therefore, being able to effectively manage and resolve conflicts is crucial to the development and upkeep of healthy relationships in all aspects of life.

Lack of conflict management in life can be caused by a variety of factors, including:

a. Communication difficulties: Conflicts can arise when a person is unable to effectively express their feelings and thoughts.
b. Lack of ability to solve problems: Conflicts tend to grow in intensity and become more challenging to manage when one party is unable to identify and resolve issues.
c. Differences in personality: Conflicts can result from personality, values, and beliefs differences, especially when people are unable to comprehend or accept each other's points of view.
d. Conflicts over power: Conflicts can begin and quickly escalate when individuals or groups vie for power.
e. Immature emotion: It may be difficult for some people to deal with conflict in a calm and rational manner because they lack emotional maturity.
f. Differing cultures: Social mistaken assumptions or absence of

mindfulness can prompt struggles between people or gatherings from various social foundations.

These are just a few of the factors that can lead to poor conflict resolution in life.

Personal and professional relationships can suffer from difficulties brought on by a lack of conflict management skills, which can result in misunderstandings, resentment, and stress. The following are some approaches that can assist individuals in improving their skills at managing conflicts:

a. Self-reflection: It is essential to effectively manage conflict to understand one's feelings, beliefs, and actions. During conflicts, individuals can learn to identify and manage their own emotions by reflecting on previous experiences and examining personal triggers.
b. Continuous listening: In conflict resolution, it is essential to listen to and comprehend the other person's point of view. It is essential to actively and without interruption listen to them and validate their thoughts and feelings.
c. Communication: Conflict resolution relies heavily on effective communication. Using "I" statements rather than "you" statements, people can learn to communicate clearly and respectfully without pointing fingers at others.
d. Problem-solving: In conflict management, it is essential to concentrate on finding a solution rather than placing blame on one another. People can collaborate to come up with a solution that both parties can live with and addresses their concerns.
e. Seek conciliation: It can be beneficial to seek the assistance of a trained third party who is able to facilitate communication and assist parties in reaching an agreement if conflicts continue.

Individuals can effectively manage conflicts and develop healthy relationships with others by developing these skills and putting them to
good use.

Kunal's lack of conflict management skills can show up in a variety of ways in life. Both personally and professionally, Kunal may have difficulty resolving conflicts, which can result in tense relationships and potentially negative outcomes.

Kunal's lack of conflict management skills could be due to the following:

a. Inadequate awareness: It may be difficult for Kunal to recognize and address his behavior because he may not be aware of how he responds to conflict situations.
b. Communication shortcomings: During conflict situations, Kunal may struggle to effectively convey his point of view, resulting in misunderstandings and escalating the situation.
c. Inability to control one's emotions: During times of conflict, Kunal might have trouble controlling his emotions, which could cause him to lash out or cause the conflict to get worse.

Kunal can take the following measures to address his lack of conflict management abilities:

a. Developing self-awareness: To better comprehend how he responds to conflict; Kunal can reflect on his own emotional triggers and communication styles.
b. Enhance communication abilities: Kunal can put effective communication strategies into practice, such as active listening,
asking questions that are open-ended and making use of "I" statements to convey his point of view.
c. Learn strategies for resolving conflicts: Kunal can learn practical conflict resolution strategies like compromise,

negotiation, and mediation from books, courses, or workshops.

d. Get professional assistance: If Kunal's lack of skills in conflict management is causing him significant problems in his personal or professional life, he might want to talk to a therapist or counselor who can help him learn these skills.

Kunal can improve his ability to handle conflicts in both his personal and professional life by taking these steps to develop his conflict management skills.

An individual's personal and professional lives can be significantly impacted if they lack conflict management skills. It has the potential to cause anxiety, strained relationships, missed opportunities, and several other negative outcomes. Having said that, it's essential to keep in mind that conflict management is a skill that can be acquired over time.

Communication, active listening, problem-solving, and coming to an agreement are all essential components of conflict management. People are better able to resolve conflicts and achieve mutually beneficial outcomes when they improve these skills. Getting training or coaching, practicing active listening, and approaching conflicts with an open mind and a willingness to compromise are all good ways to improve your ability to manage conflicts.

Recognizing that disagreements are a normal part of human interaction and cannot always be avoided is also essential. People can strengthen their relationships, increase their professional success, and improve their overall well-being by learning how to manage and resolve conflicts in a constructive and respectful manner.

30.Lack of Assertiveness

Lack of assertiveness is the inability or unwillingness to express one's own needs, desires, opinions, or boundaries in an appropriate, direct, and respectful manner in life. Poor communication, misunderstanding, resentment, and lack of respect are all possible outcomes of this in personal and professional relationships.

People who aren't assertive may find it hard to say "no" or stand up for themselves, or they may believe they don't have the right to say what they think or feel. They may also experience feelings of discomfort or anxiety when expressing themselves. On the other hand, being too assertive in one's self-expression can also result in issues, as it may come across as aggressive or disrespectful, and it can also harm relationships.

The trick is to strike a balance between being assertive and respectful in one's self-expression and considering the feelings and requirements of others.

A lack of assertiveness in life can be caused by several things, including:

a. Low self-worth: Because they doubt their abilities and are afraid of being disapproved of or rejected, people who have low self-esteem may have trouble being assertive.
b. Aversion to conflict: Some people may avoid asserting themselves for fear that doing so will result in interpersonal conflict or tension.
c. Previous experiences: Bullying or other traumatic experiences can make people feel powerless and afraid to advocate for themselves.
d. Societal or cultural norms: Individual assertiveness may be discouraged, and conformity may be emphasized in some cultures or societies.
e. Communication difficulties: Because they lack the necessary

communication skills to effectively express their thoughts and feelings, some people may struggle with assertiveness.

f. Persona of passiveness: It may be difficult for some people to be assertive and speak up for themselves because they have a passive personality.

It is essential to keep in mind that the factors that lead to a lack of assertiveness can be varied and intricate.

A lack of assertiveness can be addressed in life through a variety of methods, including:

a. Be more assertive in your communication: Practicing assertive communication is one of the best ways to become more assertive. This means being direct and respectful when expressing your needs, feelings, and thoughts. In everyday situations, like asking for a raise or expressing your needs in a relationship, you can practice assertive communication.
b. Limit yourself by setting boundaries: Being assertive requires having clear boundaries. This requires determining what you are most at ease with and what you are least at ease with and expressing this to others. You can ensure that your needs are met and that you are not exploited by setting boundaries.
c. Engage in constructive self-talk: Negative self-talk can make it difficult to be assertive. Try challenging negative thoughts like "I'm not good enough" or "Nobody cares what I think" and replacing them with ones that are more upbeat and affirming.
d. Building self-confidence: You can feel more at ease expressing your needs and standing up for yourself by improving your self-confidence. By practicing self-care, setting attainable goals, and learning new skills, you can boost your confidence.

e. Get professional assistance: You might want to think about getting help from a mental health professional if your lack of assertiveness is causing you a lot of stress or making it hard for you to get things done. You can get help from a therapist to figure out what's causing your lack of assertiveness and come up with effective ways to fix it.

Neha's lack of assertiveness in life may manifest in a variety of ways. Neha may, for instance, avoid speaking up in a group setting or feel uneasy expressing her thoughts, emotions, or requirements. She might have trouble saying "no" to people, so she might agree to things she doesn't want to do to avoid conflict or being disappointed. Over time, this can result in resentment, stress, and even burnout.

Fear of rejection, anxiety, or low self-esteem could be some of the factors that contribute to Neha's lack of assertiveness. It's possible that as a child, she was taught that it's not okay to speak her mind or that it doesn't matter what she thinks. Alternatively, she might have been taught to put the wants and opinions of other people ahead of her own.

Neha could address this by working on her self-confidence, communicating clearly, and setting boundaries. She could begin by naming her needs and values and assertively and without apologizing for them. She could also work up to more difficult situations by practicing saying "no" to smaller requests or invitations. She may also benefit from seeking assistance from a coach or therapist in developing her assertiveness skills.

Lack of assertiveness may be a difficult problem for people since it can affect many aspects of life, including successful relationships and careers. The good news is that with effort and dedication, assertiveness can be acquired and improved over time. Understanding the underlying factors that contribute to lack of assertiveness, such as fear of rejection or unfavorable results, is crucial. Self-confidence and communication skills should also be developed. Important components of assertiveness are effective communication, creating boundaries, and clearly and respectfully expressing needs and wishes.

Getting aid from dependable friends, family members, or experts like a therapist or coach can also be beneficial in dealing with this problem. People may enhance their quality of life and gain more assertiveness with hard work and perseverance.

31.Lack of Inspiration

Lack of inspiration in life is the feeling of not having the drive or motivation to pursue one's goals or take action toward fulfilling one's purpose or desires. It can result in a lack of enthusiasm, productivity, or creativity and is characterized by a sense of apathy, disinterest, or boredom. People who aren't inspired can feel like they're stuck in a rut and can't get out of their day-to-day routine. They might feel like they aren't living up to their full potential and have trouble finding meaning and purpose in their work or personal lives. Dissatisfaction, frustration, and even depression can result from this.

However, it is essential to keep in mind that feeling demotivated is a common occurrence that can affect anyone and is not always a sign of personal failure or inadequateness. It can be brought on by several internal and external factors, and it can be addressed with the right mindset and strategies.

Life's lack of inspiration can be caused by several factors, including:

a. Lack of understanding of the purpose and goals: It can be difficult for a person to find inspiration when they are unsure of their objectives and purpose in life.

b. Stress and exhaustion: A person may find it difficult to find inspiration or motivation to pursue their passions or goals when they are constantly stressed out or burned out.

c. Negative attitude: A person's inspiration can be sapped, and it can be difficult to find motivation if they have a negative mindset, such as self-doubt, fear, and cynicism.

d. Inaccessibility to new concepts: It can be difficult for someone to find creativity and inspiration if they are not exposed to novel concepts or experiences.

e. Lack of enthusiasm: It may be difficult for someone to find inspiration and motivation to pursue their objectives when they are not passionate about anything.

f. Neglecting self-care: It may be difficult for a person to find inspiration and motivation to pursue their goals when they neglect their physical, mental, and emotional well-being.
g. Factors in the environment: A person's level of inspiration can also be influenced by the surroundings in which they live, work, or socialize.

In general, a lack of motivation can have a variety of complex and individual-specific causes.

A lack of inspiration can be overcome in life in several ways, including:

a. Find new experiences to try: Experimenting with new things and meeting new people, places, and cultures can help you find inspiration.
b. Be surrounded by positive people: You can become more motivated and inspired by spending time with people who are driven and passionate.
c. Get a break: Taking a step back and giving yourself some time to rest and refuel can sometimes help spark new thoughts and ideas.
d. Take part in creative endeavors: Writing, painting, or playing music are all creative activities that can help spark new ideas and stimulate the imagination.
e. Learn from books: You can expand your knowledge and get new ideas by reading books, articles, or documentaries about topics that interest you.
f. Find inspiration in the natural world: Nature can help you think clearly and come up with new ideas.
g. Make goals: Setting attainable goals for yourself can assist in providing focus and direction, which can be inspiring.

Keep in mind that inspiration can strike at any time and can come from a variety of different sources. The key is to actively seek

inspiration in all aspects of your life and to be open to new experiences and concepts.
Natasha's lack of life inspiration can manifest in a variety of ways. Feeling unmotivated, disengaged from life, lacking a sense of direction, stuck, or unable to find meaning in one's experiences are all examples of this. Feelings of boredom, frustration, and unfulfillment can result from this.

A feeling of being disconnected from one's values and passions, negative self-talk, and limiting beliefs are just a few of the many factors that can contribute to a lack of inspiration. For Natasha, it might be helpful to think about what really excites and inspires her, what values and interests are important to her, and what she wants to accomplish in life.

There are several options for dealing with a lack of motivation. Some examples include:

a. Getting back in touch with one's passions and values: A sense of direction and purpose can be sparked by determining one's core values and priorities.
b. Having clear objectives: A sense of forward momentum and motivation can be facilitated by setting specific, attainable goals.
c. Engaging in activities that are creative or challenging: Experimenting with new things or engaging in activities that test one's abilities can help one feel inspired and excited.
d. Mindfulness and self-compassion practice: Being kind and compassionate to oneself, practicing mindfulness on a regular basis, and cultivating a sense of calm and ease can help to cultivate a greater sense of motivation and fulfillment.
e. Getting help: To investigate and address a lack of inspiration, working with a coach or therapist can provide support and direction.

Natasha can begin to feel more engaged, motivated, and fulfilled in her life by addressing a lack of inspiration.

People who are feeling stuck, unmotivated, or out of direction may face significant difficulties due to a lack of inspiration. Stress, burnout, a lack of purpose or direction, as well as feelings of overwhelm or uncertainty, are all potential causes.

The good news is that overcoming a lack of inspiration and finding new sources of motivation and direction in one's life is possible with a variety of strategies and methods. Setting attainable goals, seeking out new experiences and challenges, surrounding oneself with positive and supportive people, and participating in activities that bring joy and fulfillment are some of these strategies.

In addition, it can be beneficial to engage in self-reflection and investigate what truly inspires and matters to oneself. Identifying one's values, strengths, and interests and finding ways to align one's daily life and activities with them can be part of this. It can also be beneficial to seek inspiration from other people, whether through mentors, books, podcasts, or other means.

In the end, the only way to get over a lack of inspiration is to be willing to be open to new concepts and experiences, to try new things and take chances, and to take on the challenges and opportunities that life throws at you. By doing this, people can discover new sources of inspiration and motivation and lead lives that are more meaningful and satisfying.

32.Lack of Initiative

Lack of initiative in life refers to a person's inability to initiate or take action on their own. It's not being able to act or take the first step toward changing or achieving a goal. People who lack initiative may experience feelings of being stuck or unsure of what to do, making it difficult for them to take on new challenges and make decisions. Because it can result in missed opportunities, unfulfilled potential, and insufficient progress toward one's goals, lack of initiative can be a significant roadblock to personal and professional development. It can also have an impact on relationships and cause feelings of helplessness, frustration, and low self-esteem.

However, it is essential to keep in mind that a lack of initiative is not a permanent personality trait and that individuals can develop and improve their initiative with effort and practice.

Life's lack of initiative can be caused by a variety of factors, including:

a. Fear of Loss: Because they don't want to be criticized for their efforts or making a mistake, people who are afraid of failing may be reluctant to act.
b. A lack of self-esteem: People who lack self-assurance may be less likely to take the initiative and may feel intimidated by new challenges.
c. Lack of guidance: People may be unsure of what actions to take or where to focus their efforts if they do not have a clear sense of purpose or direction.
d. A lack of drive: Apathy and a general lack of interest in taking initiative or pursuing new opportunities can result from a lack of motivation.
e. Favorite Habits: If someone is overly content with their current situation and doesn't want to risk the possibility of change, they might be reluctant to take the initiative.

f. Past Negative Experiences: People may be reluctant to take the initiative and pursue new opportunities because of previous experiences of failure, rejection, or disappointment.
g. Lack of Assistance: People may be discouraged from taking the initiative and pursuing their objectives if they lack the support of family, friends, or colleagues.
h. Procrastination: A lack of initiative and missed opportunities can result from delaying decisions or tasks.
i. Problems with the mind: A person's energy and motivation can be sapped by mental health conditions like depression or anxiety, which can result in a lack of initiative.
j. Physical Problems: A person's energy and motivation can be impacted by physical health issues, which can result in a lack of initiative.

To effectively address a lack of initiative, it is essential to pinpoint its root cause.

The following steps can be taken to address lack of initiative in life:

a. Set clear objectives: The first step in taking the initiative is to set clear, attainable goals. This provides a sense of direction and focus as well as a goal to work toward.
b. Divide tasks into manageable steps: Procrastination can result from large and complex tasks that are intimidating. Tasks can be less overwhelming and easier to complete when broken down into smaller, more manageable steps.
c. Make a strategy: It can be easier to take the initiative if you have a plan that lays out the steps you need to take to reach your goals. This may be of assistance in ensuring that the individual is aware of what needs to be done and when.

d. Prioritize: To ensure that the most crucial tasks are completed first, it is essential to assign tasks a priority. This helps keep the focus on the task at hand and prevents distractions.
e. Make a move: It is essential to act and begin working toward the objective at some point. Small steps toward the goal can encourage more initiative and help build momentum.
f. Develop self-control: When taking initiative, self-discipline is essential. Being persistent in your pursuit of the objective, adhering to a schedule, setting priorities, and avoiding distractions are all part of this.
g. Seek assistance: A lack of confidence or a fear of failure can sometimes cause a lack of initiative. A mentor, friend, or family member can encourage you and help you feel more confident.

Individuals can overcome lack of initiative and move toward achieving their objectives by taking these steps.

Joe's lack of initiative can manifest in a variety of ways. Joe, for instance, may believe that he is stuck or unable to advance in his life or career. It's possible that he lacks the drive to achieve his goals or take on new challenges. He may also struggle with procrastination, frequently delaying or failing to complete tasks.

Fear of failure or rejection, a lack of confidence or self-esteem, feeling overwhelmed or unsure of what to do, or simply feeling unmotivated or disengaged are all potential causes of Joe's lack of initiative.

Joe's lack of initiative can be addressed by determining the root cause of his lack of motivation and devising a strategy to address it. This might entail making smaller, more manageable goals, breaking larger tasks down into smaller steps, looking for mentorship or support from other people, and recognizing small victories along the way. Self-care practices like exercising, getting enough sleep, and eating a healthy diet may also help Joe feel more motivated and energetic.

A difficult problem for people to deal with in life is a lack of initiative because it can impede their progress and success. However, it is essential to keep in mind that this obstacle can be overcome with the right mindset, strategies, and support.

Setting attainable goals, breaking larger goals down into smaller, more manageable steps, seeking accountability or support from friends, family, or a coach, finding inspiration and motivation through hobbies or interests, and practicing self-reflection and self-compassion are some possible solutions to dealing with lack of initiative.

Additionally, it is essential to identify and address any underlying reasons for the lack of initiative, such as self-doubt, fear, or a lack of direction or clarity. People can cultivate a sense of purpose and the drive to take action and advance in their lives by working on self-awareness and growth mindset.

33.Lack of Goal Setting

Lack of goal setting in life is the absence of clear and specific goals that a person wants to achieve in various areas of their life, such as personal, professional, financial, or health-related goals. A person who doesn't set goals may feel lost, unfulfilled, or without a sense of purpose. This can make them feel unmotivated, low on self-esteem, and unhappy with their life. It can be hard to decide on a plan of action or a list of priorities without clear goals, which can waste time and resources. Also, if there are no clear goals, it can be hard to track progress and figure out when milestones have been reached. This makes it hard to track success and know when to change course.

Failure to set goals in life can be caused by a variety of factors. Common reasons include:

a. Clarity deficiency: It may be difficult for someone to set goals if they are unsure of their values or what they want to accomplish.
b. Aversion to failure: Fear of failure can prevent some people from setting goals, which can cause feelings of failure or disappointment.
c. A lack of drive: A person may not see the point in setting a goal if they are not motivated to accomplish something.
d. Procrastination: Because they are feeling overwhelmed or unsure of where to begin, some people put off setting goals.
e. A lack of self-assurance: People who lack self-confidence may be hesitant to set goals because they believe they won't be able to achieve them.
f. Lack of assistance: It can be difficult for someone to set and achieve goals if they don't have support from friends, family, or peers.

g. External variables: A person's ability to concentrate on setting goals can sometimes be hindered by external factors like health or financial concerns.

These are just a few of the reasons why people don't set goals for themselves in life.

There are a few things you can do to fix the problem of not setting goals for yourself in life:

a. Identify your priorities and values: You can set goals that are in line with your values if you know what matters most to you.
b. Begin small: Start by establishing attainable short-term objectives that can assist you in gaining momentum and confidence. After completing these, you can move on to more important long-term objectives.
c. Make a strategy: Divide your objectives into SMART goals which are specific, measurable, achievable, relevant, and time bound. You'll be able to stay organized and focused on your objectives with this.
d. Get assistance: Ask someone you trust for assistance and support in accomplishing your objectives after sharing it with them. You can also think about engaging with a coach or mentor who can help you create and achieve goals.
e. Recognize your accomplishments: Celebrate your progress and achievements along the way. This may assist you in maintaining your enthusiasm and commitment to achieving your objectives.
f. Be adaptable: Be willing to make any necessary adjustments to your objectives considering shifting priorities and conditions. Flexibility is a necessary component of achieving and setting effective goals.

g. Learn from failure: Recognize that failures and setbacks are a normal part of setting goals. Take advantage of these experiences to gain knowledge, adapt your strategy, and increase your chances of success.

Let's take Jonathan as an example, who doesn't set goals for his life. Without a clear idea of what he wants to accomplish or how to get there, Jonathan may feel aimless and lost. Feelings of frustration, lack of motivation, and difficulty making decisions can result from this lack of clarity.

Jonathan may have trouble managing his time and setting priorities, which could result in a lack of progress in his personal and professional lives. Additionally, he may have difficulty measuring his success or feeling proud of his accomplishments.

Jonathan can begin by reflecting on his values, interests, and long-term goals to overcome this lack of goal setting. He can then begin working toward specific, measurable objectives that are in line with his life's vision. Jonathan might find it helpful to break down more ambitious objectives into smaller, more manageable steps, to set deadlines, and to hold himself accountable for progress.

Jonathan can also benefit from seeking mentorship, direction, or support from people who have set and achieved goals in the past. This could be accomplished through programs for professional development, individual coaching, or simply seeking advice from friends or coworkers.

In the end, making it a habit to set goals and keep track of progress can help Jonathan feel more motivated, fulfilled, and purposeful in both his personal and professional lives.

A lack of goal setting can result in a lack of life satisfaction, direction, and purpose. It can be hard to know where to put your time, effort, and resources if your goals are unclear. A sense of stagnation, unfulfillment, and lack of progress can result from this.

Keep in mind that goal setting is a skill that can be learned through practice. Identifying what you want to accomplish and why it is important to you is the first step. You can then plan to achieve your goals by breaking them down into smaller, more manageable steps. It is also essential to monitor your progress on a regular basis and make any necessary adjustments to your plan.

Incorporating daily practices like mindfulness and reflection into your life can also help you become more self-aware and clearer about your goals in life. Keep in mind that setting goals is an ongoing process and that it is never too late to begin working toward a life that is more meaningful and fulfilling.

34.Lack of Decision Making

Lack of decision making is a reference to the inability or difficulty of making feasible and optimal decisions in various spheres of life. Individual, academic, or professional decisions made in this manner could have a variety of negative effects, such as missed opportunities, uncertainty, and less certainty. Individuals who lack critical thinking skills may struggle to gather and research information, weigh the benefits and drawbacks of numerous options, and ultimately make a decision that is consistent with their goals and values. They might also struggle with feeling overwhelmed by the variety of options available to them or the fear of making a bad choice. It is critical to take note that thinking abilities can be created and improved with training and direction.

There are a few likely foundations for an absence of critical thinking abilities, including:

a. Fear of making wrong decision: This can prompt overthinking, investigation loss of motion, and hesitation.
b. Absence of confidence: This can make it hard to pay attention to your gut feelings and go with a firm choice.
c. Absence of experience: Without experience, it tends to be trying to know how to settle on a decent choice, or to trust your judgment.
d. Cognitive biases: These are mental easy routes that can prompt defective navigation, for example, tendency to look for predetermined feedback (searching out data that upholds your current convictions) or the sunk expense deception (proceeding to put resources into a faltering venture since you've previously contributed time or assets).
e. Feelings: Compelling feelings like fear, anxiety, or anger can cloud your judgment and make it challenging to think obviously and settle on a decent choice.
f. Environmental variables: Distressing or diverting conditions

can make it challenging to focus and use sound judgment.

g. Absence of data or analysis: Not having sufficient data or neglecting to break down it appropriately can make it difficult to make a well-informed decision.

These are only a couple of expected reasons for lack of decision-making skills. It's vital to take note that everybody's circumstances are exceptional, and there might be different elements that add to this issue.

The following are some possible solutions to dealing with life's decision-making difficulties:

a. Determine the source: It is essential to identify the problem's underlying cause to improve decision-making abilities. It could be because you don't know enough, you're afraid of failing, or you don't feel confident. Finding a solution becomes easier once the cause is identified.
b. Collect details: Obtaining as much information as possible is one strategy for improving decision-making abilities. Before deciding, it is essential to analyze the data and gather pertinent information.
c. Analyze the benefits and drawbacks: Before deciding, it is essential to weigh the advantages and disadvantages of each option after gathering the relevant information. Think about the potential advantages and disadvantages of each choice.
d. Get help from others: It is always beneficial to seek guidance and advice from other people, particularly from those who have experience making decisions that are comparable to yours. They can provide valuable insights and a new point of view.
e. Practice making decisions: The ability to make decisions is one that can be learned through practice. Start by making simple choices before moving on to more difficult ones. As a

result, confidence will grow, and decision-making skills will improve.

f. Think back on previous choices: A great way to learn from mistakes and improving your ability to make decisions in the future is to look back at decisions made in the past and how they turned out. Understanding what worked and what didn't work, as well as what could have been done differently, is essential.
g. Boost self-assurance: Improved decision-making abilities necessitate confidence building. Having a growth mindset, focusing on one's own development, and developing a positive self-image are all ways to boost confidence and make better decisions.

A person's life can be affected in a variety of ways by a lack of decision-making skills, and these effects can vary depending on the individual's circumstances. Shyam, for instance, may struggle both personally and professionally because of his inability to make well-thought-out decisions. Shyam may find it difficult to make important decisions in his personal life, like where to live, what career path to take, or who to marry. He may feel indecisive, uncertain, or overwhelmed by the options available to him, and this can lead to procrastination, anxiety, or missed opportunities. Shyam may have trouble making good decisions in his professional life, like whether to take on a new project, how to divide resources, or how to deal with disagreements with coworkers. He may be hesitant to take risks or lack confidence in his ability to make wise decisions, which can lead to missed opportunities, lower productivity, or even job loss. A person's overall ability to effectively navigate life can be limited by a lack of decision-making skills, which can result in missed opportunities, decreased confidence, and increased stress and anxiety.

As a result, Shyam must work on improving his decision-making abilities. This might entail practicing techniques to make clear his values and priorities, gathering information, thinking about a lot of options, weighing the benefits and drawbacks of each one, and then deciding based on what he thinks is best. He might also benefit from speaking with mentors, coaches, or trusted family and friends for advice and support. Shyam can improve his ability to make sound and effective choices that are in line with his goals and values and ultimately lead to a life that is more satisfying and successful by improving his decision-making skills.

A person's inability to make decisions can be a major roadblock in their life. Indecisiveness, poor choices, and missed opportunities are all possible outcomes. However, it is a skill that can be learned and honed through practice.

It's important to remember that making decisions is a process rather than a single action. Better decision-making can be achieved by taking the time to consider options, gather information, weigh advantages and disadvantages, and consider potential outcomes.

Understanding the root causes of poor decision-making, such as a lack of information, fear, or impulsivity, is also critical. People may gain self-assurance in their ability to make decisions if these issues are addressed.

In addition, developing this crucial life skill can be helped by looking for mentors or role models who are adept decision-makers and reading about decision-making strategies and methods.

Overall, even though having poor decision-making skills can be difficult, it is not impossible to master it. Individuals can learn to make better choices and ultimately achieve greater life success and fulfillment with effort and dedication to personal growth.

35.Lack of Risk Taking

Lack of risk-taking in life is the tendency to avoid taking chances or risks in various aspects of life, such as personal relationships, career, finances, and other areas. Even if they have the potential for positive outcomes, people who lack risk-taking tend to be extremely cautious and prefer to avoid making choices that may have a negative impact. A persistent lack of risk-taking can result in missed opportunities and a failure to realize one's full potential, even though it is reasonable to take precautions to avoid negative outcomes. This can lead to stagnation and a lack of personal development, which can have a long-term effect on one's personal and professional lives.

Life's lack of risk-taking can be caused by several factors. The most typical examples include:

a. Aversion to failure: Fear of failure is one of the most common factors that prevent people from taking risks. Because they believe that failing will be too painful or embarrassing, people who are afraid of failing frequently avoid taking risks.
b. Low self-worth: People who have low self-esteem frequently lack the courage to try new things. It's possible that they don't have enough faith in themselves to try something new.
c. Lack of experience: A lack of confidence in taking risks can result from a lack of experience in a particular field. People may doubt their ability to succeed if they have no prior experience or knowledge.
d. Perfectionism: Risk-taking may be avoided by perfectionists who are afraid of making mistakes. As a result, they may be reluctant to try new things, take risks, or venture outside of their comfort zones.
e. Previous experiences: Negative past experiences, such as setbacks or failures, can prevent people from taking risks in the future. They might be afraid of making the same mistakes

again or they might simply lack the self-assurance to try again.

f. Pressure from outside: A lack of risk-taking can also be caused by external pressures like societal expectations, peer pressure, or pressure from family or friends. Even if it means avoiding risks, people may feel pressure to conform to what others expect of them.

A variety of factors, including fear, low self-esteem, lack of experience, perfectionism, past experiences, and external pressures, can all contribute to a lack of risk-taking.

One can overcome their lack of risk-taking in life by employing the following methods:

a. Starting small: A good way to build confidence and get used to the idea of taking risks is to take small risks. For instance, taking a different route to work or trying a new restaurant are small risks that can help build confidence.
b. Create a strategy: Taking a risk can be less costly if you have a strategy in place. Anxiety can be reduced, and confidence raised by planning and contemplating possible outcomes.
c. Accept failure: Taking risks is inevitably accompanied by failure. Instead of viewing failure as a sign of weakness or incompetence, it's important to see it as an opportunity to learn and develop.
d. Be surrounded by supportive people: Being surrounded by friends and family who are there for you can inspire you to try new things. Talking about your worries and fears with someone
who understands can also be helpful.
e. Make mindfulness a habit: Self-awareness and anxiety can be reduced through mindfulness, making it easier to take risks.

f. Challenging negative thought: Taking risks can be significantly hampered by negative thinking. Building confidence and reducing anxiety can both be aided by challenging negative thoughts and reframe them in a more positive light.

Individuals can begin to pursue their goals and dreams by putting these strategies into practice and conquering their fear of taking risks.

Life's lack of risk-taking refers to a fear of failure, uncertainty, or discomfort that prevents people from trying new things or taking risks. This may show up in a variety of life areas, including relationships, career, personal growth, and more, for Sumati.

Because of a need for stability and predictability, a lack of self-confidence, or a fear of failure, Sumati may avoid taking risks and exploring new opportunities. This can result in less life satisfaction and fulfillment as well as missed opportunities for personal and professional development. Sumati may avoid asking for a raise or promotion, taking on challenging projects, or pursuing new job opportunities in her career. She might avoid trying out new things, meeting new people, taking on new responsibilities, or expressing her wants and needs in a relationship in her personal life.

Sumati can work on increasing her self-confidence, challenging her limiting beliefs, and reframe failure as an opportunity for growth and learning to overcome her lack of risk-taking. She can begin by setting modest, attainable objectives and gradually stepping outside of her comfort zone. She can also get assistance from family, friends, or a therapist which will help her to become more courageous and resilient in the face of challenges and uncertainty.

Another example is Rahul, a fresh college graduate, who has received a job offer from a reputable organization. He is hesitant to accept the job offer though because he is anxious about relocating away from his hometown and into a new place. He feels secure in his routine and surroundings right now, so the thought of taking a chance by beginning a new career in a different place makes him anxious. Rahul is unable to take advantage of the fantastic opportunity for professional and personal development that the job offer presents because he is afraid to take a gamble. He finds it difficult to decide and advance in his job as a result.

People who do not take risks in life may be prevented from taking advantage of opportunities and achieving their objectives. While there are valid reasons to be cautious and steer clear of unnecessary risks, excessive fear and risk avoidance can result in missed opportunities and a life filled with regret. It's critical to find a middle ground between taking calculated risks and acting recklessly.

A variety of factors, including a lack of self-confidence, a desire for safety and comfort, fear of failure, and negative experiences in the past, can contribute to a lack of risk-taking. However, individuals can improve their risk-taking capacity and decision-making abilities with effort and practice. Individuals can develop their confidence and ability to take calculated risks by seeking out new experiences, setting goals that are realistic, developing a support system, and learning from previous failures.

36.Lack of Trust

Lack of trust is the inability or unwillingness of an individual to believe in the honesty, dependability, or sincerity of another individual or group. It can manifest itself in a variety of ways, including skepticism, cynicism, or a general sense of distrust towards other people. People who lack trust may have trouble, among other things, developing close relationships, disclosing personal information, delegating tasks to others, and working together with coworkers. Negative past experiences, such as being betrayed, lied to, or deceived by others, can lead to a lack of trust. Cultural, social, or environmental factors that foster a sense of insecurity or hostility towards particular groups can also have an impact. A lack of trust in others can also be caused by psychological issues like anxiety, low self-esteem, or trauma.

In general, a lack of faith in life can make it difficult for a person to form meaningful relationships and advance toward their personal or professional objectives. To build relationships with other people which are more satisfying and positive, it is essential to address any underlying issues that may be causing this lack of trust. A lack of faith in life can be brought on by a variety of factors, including:

a. Previous experiences: It may be difficult for someone to trust others in the future if they have been betrayed or hurt in the past.
b. Fear of being vulnerable: It can be hard for some people to open and be vulnerable, which can make it hard for them to trust other people.
c. Social or cultural factors: Due to social norms and expectations,
it may be more challenging to trust others in some cultures.
d. Character traits: Due to their personality, some people may be naturally more skeptical or have a harder time trusting others.

e. Issues with mental health: A lack of trust in others can be caused by mental health issues like anxiety, depression, or post-traumatic stress disorder (PTSD).
f. Communication problems: Poor communication in relationships can lead to misunderstandings and a breakdown in trust.
g. Conflicts not resolved: Relationship trust can be eroded by unresolved conflicts if not resolved timely.
h. Transparency issues: A lack of trust can result when people are not open and honest about their intentions or actions.
i. Negative media and news: Some people may lose faith in others after being exposed to negative media or news.

These are only a handful of the numerous possible reasons why someone could lack trust in life.

It can be hard to deal with a lack of faith in life, but there are a few ways to help. Consider the following possible solutions:

a. Determine the root of distrust: It is essential to comprehend the source of the distrust. Is it a lack of self-assurance, trauma, or previous experiences? You can address the issue once you know where it came from.
b. Seek treatment: It can be difficult to overcome a lack of trust on your own at times. A therapist can guide you on how to build trust with others, develop coping strategies, and work through your emotions.
c. Make yourself vulnerable: It takes a lot of vulnerability to build trust. Sharing means sharing your thoughts, feelings, and experiences with others, even when it's uncomfortable. You may show people you have faith in them by being vulnerable with them and letting them see a vulnerable side of you.

d. Smaller risks: Taking small risks is often necessary for building trust. This could mean asking for help when you need it, sharing something intimate with a trusted individual, or relying on another person to keep a promise. You can gradually build trust with other people by taking small risks.
e. Openly communicate: The foundation of trust is communication. When you talk to other people, be honest and open with them. Express your worries and doubts in an open and respectful manner. You may be able to strengthen your relationships and establish trust with this.
f. Have Patience: Be patient since trust-building takes time. While you attempt to establish trust, it is crucial to be patient with both you and other people. Keep in mind that developing trust is a process and takes time.

To deal with life's lack of trust, these might be some options. Understanding that it takes time, effort, and a willingness to be vulnerable to build trust is essential. You can build relationships and experiences that are more powerful and meaningful if you work on trusting yourself and others.

A person named Karan who lacks trust in life might also have trouble trusting those around him. It could be because he has felt mistrust and skepticism in the past because he has been betrayed, hurt, or let down by someone he trusted. Alternately, it's possible that Karan grew up in an environment where people close to him, like his parents, friends, or family, constantly failed or betrayed him, making it hard for him to build trust. Because he may constantly feel the need to exert control over the situation or avoid being hurt, Karan may have trouble forming new relationships, maintaining those he already has, and working as part of a team. His low self-esteem and lack of confidence may also make it difficult for him to make decisions and take risks.

Karan can take small steps to restore trust in others to overcome his lack of trust. He can begin by considering his previous experiences and determining the root of his mistrust. He might find it helpful to talk to a therapist or a trusted friend about any unresolved emotions or traumatic experiences.

Karan should also concentrate on honing his effective communication techniques and being open-minded and honest with others. He can begin by being open and honest about his feelings and views, as well as by outlining his expectations. As a result, both his self-confidence and that of others will increase, and his connections will become stronger.

Instead of being overly pessimistic or skeptical, Karan can also try to focus on the positive aspects of people and situations. He may be able to develop relationships with those around him that are more trustworthy and supportive if he adopts a more upbeat outlook on life.

A person's relationships and overall well-being can be significantly impacted by a lack of trust. It can cause feelings of loneliness, isolation, and insecurity. However, it is essential to keep in mind that trust can be reestablished over time and that there are several strategies for gaining trust in oneself and others.

Beginning with self-reflection and identifying any personal beliefs or experiences from the past that may be contributing to a lack of trust is an essential step. In relationships, practicing vulnerability and communicating openly and honestly about one's needs and concerns can also be beneficial.

Getting help from a therapist or counselor can also help you learn how to build trust and deal with underlying issues. It is possible to overcome a lack of trust and cultivate relationships that are more fulfilling as well as a stronger sense of self with time and effort.

37.Lack of Integrity

Lack of integrity in life is an individual's lack of honesty, ethics, and moral principles in their behavior. It implies that a person does not hold themselves accountable for their actions and does not keep their promises. It can manifest itself in a variety of ways, including lying, cheating, stealing, breaking promises, and failing to protect confidential information. Because it contributes to the development of trust, respect, and credibility, integrity is an essential component of a person's character. A person's lack of integrity can cause problems in their relationships, damage to their reputation, and other problems.

In life, a lack of integrity can be brought on by a variety of factors. Some possibilities include:

a. Fear: People who are afraid of losing something, like power, money, or relationships, may compromise their integrity.
b. Pressure: People can feel as though they need to compromise their integrity to meet expectations when they are under pressure from others, such as their boss, peers, or family.
c. Low self-worth: People with low self-esteem may compromise their integrity in the pursuit of success because they may believe that they are not good enough to achieve their objectives without compromising on quality.
d. Insufficient accountability: People who lack accountability may not feel obligated to act with integrity because they do not feel responsible for their actions.
e. Rationalization: Even when they act in a way that goes against their values or principles, people can justify their actions and come to the conclusion that they are justified.
f. Inadequate awareness: It's possible that some people are unaware of what integrity is or how their actions affect it.
g. Previous experiences: People can become jaded or cynical because of past experiences like betrayal or disappointment,

leading them to believe that everyone is dishonest and that acting with integrity is pointless.

h. Environment: A person's surroundings can sometimes contribute to a lack of integrity. For instance, working in a competitive industry where everyone is vying for position can give the impression that cutting corners is the norm.

A lack of integrity can be caused by a variety of factors, some of which depend on the individual and their circumstances.

It can be challenging to deal with a lack of integrity in life, but it is not impossible. Consider the following possible solutions:

a. Identify the areas in which you lack integrity: Look at yourself and your professional and personal lives to see if there are any areas in which you are not being truthful or living up to your values. This is the first step. Determine specific instances and actions in which you have violated your integrity.
b. Accept responsibility for what you did: Accept responsibility for your actions and admit your mistakes. Although this is an essential step in moving forward, it can be a challenging process.
c. Create a personal code of conduct: Take some time to write down your personal ethics and values, which you can use to guide you through difficult decisions.
d. Seek the advice of a dependable mentor or counselor: You might want to think about seeking advice from someone who can give you an objective perspective and assist you in creating a strategy for enhancing your integrity.
e. Be surrounded by trustworthy people: Look for friends and coworkers who live their lives with integrity in mind. As you work to improve your own integrity, these people can be role models for you and support.

f. Transparency and honesty are essential: In your interactions with other people, make it a conscious effort to be open and honest. This could entail making mistakes, telling the truth in difficult situations, and placing transparency at the top of your priorities in both your personal and professional relationships.
g. Set a goal to constantly improve yourself: Integrity development and upkeep are lifelong endeavors. Make a commitment to continuous self-improvement by striving to live in accordance with your values and principles and constantly evaluating your actions and decisions.

It is essential to keep in mind that developing integrity is a journey, and implementing these solutions fully may require time and effort. You can, however, begin to live a life that is more authentic and satisfying by taking proactive steps to address a lack of integrity.

A person's lack of integrity can have serious personal and professional repercussions. It could imply that Emma lacks a firm moral code and has trouble making ethical or honest decisions. Others may not trust her because she may not be trustworthy. Additionally, she may have difficulty taking responsibility for her actions and be more likely to lie.

A lack of strong values or principles, a desire to fit in or be liked, or a lack of accountability are all potential causes of lack of integrity. Additionally, Emma may have been rewarded in the past for dishonest or unethical behavior, which may have fueled that behavior.

Emma could focus on developing a strong sense of personal values and principles that she can use as a guide for her decision-making to address a lack of integrity. She could also work on taking responsibility for her mistakes and being more accountable for her actions. She can also improve her integrity by seeking feedback from others and being open to constructive criticism.

Emma could also benefit from looking for trustworthy role models and learning from their example. Emma may also be able to improve her self-awareness and make positive changes in her life by participating in activities like meditation or journaling that support personal development and self-reflection.

Integrity issues can have major repercussions for both the offender and others around them. Integrity-challenged individuals may find it difficult to build enduring connections and may find it more difficult to win others' respect and trust. They might also be more likely to make immoral or unethical choices, which could have a negative impact on society or the law. It's crucial to remember that everyone has the capacity to make errors or exercise poor judgement.

Becoming more self-aware and contemplative, recognizing the areas where one's actions may not be in line with their ideals, and taking action to solve those concerns are the keys to developing integrity. This may entail asking for help and direction from dependable friends, family members, or experts, such a therapist or counsellor.

Throughout time, one's integrity can also be strengthened by committing to making moral decisions and strengthening one's sense of personal accountability. People can establish a reputation for themselves as trustworthy and dependable individuals in both their personal and professional lives by prioritizing honesty, transparency, and respect in all facets of life.

38.Lack of Community Involvement

Lack of community involvement is when a person or group of people do not actively participate in activities that are meant to benefit the community. It could be interpreted as a failure to take responsibility for the problems that affect the community or as a lack of interest or concern for its well-being. This can appear in changed ways, like not chipping in, not going to local gatherings, or not supporting local area-based associations or drives. Participation in the community is important because it helps to build a stronger, more cohesive community as well as a sense of social connectedness and belonging. People are more likely to be aware of the problems and needs in their community and to act on them when they are involved in it. As people come together to work toward a common objective, community involvement can also provide a sense of purpose and fulfillment.

Individuals' lack of community involvement can be attributed to a variety of factors, including the following:

a. Inadequate awareness: It's possible that some people are unaware of the opportunities to get involved in their community. They might not be aware of local events or organizations, or they might not be aware of the advantages of participating in the community.
b. Limitations on time: It's possible that busy people won't have time to get involved in their community. This could be because of work, family obligations, or other tasks that take up time.
c. Personal problems: Some individuals may be unable to participate in their community due to personal issues. They may be unable to participate in community activities due to personal challenges, mental health issues, or other issues.
d. A lack of drive: It's possible that some people lack the drive to get involved in their community. It's possible that they don't

see the value in it or that they don't care about the activities that are
available.

e. Social phobia: If you're shy or introverted, getting involved in your community might make you feel anxious. They may experience social anxiety, making it challenging for them to participate in community activities.

It's important to remember that these are just a few possible reasons why some people don't get involved in the community. There could be other reasons as well. There are a few actions a person can take to become more involved in their community if they are struggling with a lack of involvement:

a. Find your interests: Identifying activities and interests that you enjoy is a good way to get involved in the community. Participating in community events, joining a sports or hobby club, or volunteering at a local charity are all examples of this.
b. Possibilities for research: Research local organizations and events that align with your interests after determining your interests. Finding volunteers or participants who are a good fit can take some time due to the numerous organizations and groups that frequently require volunteers or participants.
c. Connecting with others: Reaching out to other people is often necessary for community involvement. This could mean contacting volunteer coordinators at local organizations or introducing yourself at community events.
d. Make a promise: Make a commitment to involve yourself in opportunities that interests you once you have found it. This could entail regularly attending events or committing to a regular volunteer schedule.
e. Keep involved: Engaging in community activities requires ongoing effort. Be sure to keep in touch with the people and

organizations you're involved with and keep looking for new ways to get involved.

It is possible to become more involved in the community and have a positive effect on the world around you by taking these steps. Individuals' lack of community involvement can manifest in a variety of ways, and the reasons for it can vary. Olivia may not participate in activities that support or benefit her local community, such as volunteering at a local shelter or participating in community clean-up events, because she lacks community involvement. These factors could be to blame for this lack of involvement:

a. Inadequate awareness: It's possible that Olivia is unaware of the opportunities to participate in her community. It's possible that she doesn't know about any local organizations or volunteer opportunities.
b. A lack of drive: Despite being aware of the opportunities to participate in her community, Olivia might not be motivated to do so. This could be because she doesn't want to get involved in the community, she feels like she has too many other responsibilities or commitments, or she just doesn't see the value in putting her time and energy into community activities.
c. Shyness or social anxiety: Olivia may experience social anxiety or discomfort, making it challenging for her to attend events and meet new people.
d. Time constraints: The majority of Olivia 's time may be consumed by work, school, or family obligations.

Olivia could try below options to address these issues and encourage greater community involvement:

a. Examine organizations in the area: Olivia could do some research to find the events and organizations in her community that resonate with her values and interests. This could be done by doing research on the internet, talking to friends and family, or going to a community center in the area.

b. Begin small: Olivia could begin by volunteering for a short time or attending a small event. She might become more at ease with the idea of community involvement because of this, and
her level of participation might gradually rise as a result.
c. Set attainable goals: Olivia could set goals for herself that work with her limited time and energy by volunteering once a month or once every three months, for example.
d. Focus on the advantages: Olivia could keep in mind the advantages of participating in the community, such as the opportunity to meet new people, acquire new skills, and have a positive effect on the community.
e. Seek assistance: Olivia could get help from friends or family who are active in their community, or she could join online communities or forums where she can meet people who are interested in the same things as her. If she struggles with social anxiety or any other mental health issues that might be hindering her participation, she might also want to talk to a professional.

Lack of community participation can cause a person to feel alone and cut off from society, which can have a detrimental effect on their wellbeing and quality of life. It can prevent people from taking advantage of chances for professional development, networking, and making a positive impact in the world. There are numerous opportunities to get engaged and give back to one's community, including volunteering for regional organizations, going to neighborhood events, joining clubs, or just mingling with neighbors and other community members. People can build stronger connections with others, gain a sense of purpose, have a beneficial effect on the world by involving themselves in the community and making a positive impact on the world around them.

39.Fear of Failure

Fear of failure is a common human emotion, an intense sense of anxiety, apprehension, or worry about not being able to achieve a particular goal or desired outcome. This fear can be brought on by a variety of things, including personal insecurities, a lack of confidence in oneself, negative experiences with failure in the past, social pressures, and expectations that are too high. Due to a belief that they will not succeed or that they will be harshly judged if they fail, people who experience a fear of failure frequently struggle to take risks or pursue new opportunities. Because the fear of failing reaffirms a person's reluctance to try new things or take on challenges they perceive as risky or uncertain, this can result in a self-defeating avoidance cycle. A person may experience feelings of helplessness, hopelessness, and low self-esteem when this fear grows to the point where it prevents them from functioning in their personal or professional life.

There is a wide range of factors that can contribute to a person's fear of failure, including the following:

a. Previous experiences: Fear of failure in the future can be exacerbated by negative feedback or previous experiences with failure. A person may be more likely to fear failure in the future if they have experienced significant failures or negative experiences in the past.
b. Perfectionism: Fear of failing can also be exacerbated by a need to be perfect. A person may fear failure because they view it as a personal mistake or flaw when they hold themselves to high standards and expect perfection in everything they do.
c. Influence from others: Fear of failure can also be brought on by pressure to achieve or meet certain expectations from others, like parents, peers, or bosses. A person may experience anxiety or fear that they will not be able to meet

the expectations that have been set for them because of this pressure.

d. Low self-worth: Fear of failure can also be brought on by a lack
of confidence or low self-esteem. A person may be more likely to avoid taking risks and fear failure if they don't believe in their ability to succeed.

e. Issues with mental health: Fear of failure can also be exacerbated by mental health issues like depression or anxiety. A person may experience a sense of fear or anxiety because of these conditions, making it difficult for them to try new things or take risks.

It is essential to keep in mind that anxiety about failing is a normal human emotion that can affect anyone. It's not necessarily a sign of weakness or a character flaw; rather, it's something that many people go through on a regular basis.

Fear of failure can be overcome in several ways, including:

a. Change your perspective: Try to reframe failure as an opportunity for learning rather than a negative outcome. Accept that failure is a normal part of learning and that everyone fails at some point.
b. Set attainable goals: You can boost your self-assurance by setting attainable goals that are in line with your abilities.
c. Divide tasks into manageable steps: If you break down difficult or overwhelming tasks into smaller, more manageable steps, you may find that they become less intimidating and that you gain momentum toward your objectives.
d. Seek assistance: It is always helpful to surround yourself with supportive people who encourage you to take chances and learn from your mistakes. Look for mentors, friends, or family

members who can give you advice and support in a constructive way.

e. Make time for yourself: You can better manage your fear of failure by taking care of your physical and mental health, which in turn can help you build resilience and control stress.
f. Make a move: Acting and facing your worries is sometimes the greatest approach to overcome fear of failing. Begin with tiny, acceptable risks and work your way up, giving yourself credit for each step you take.

Managing fear of failure can be made easier with one or more of these options. It is essential to keep in mind that every person at some point experiences fear and self-doubt, and that seeking assistance or support can be an essential step toward overcoming these feelings.

Let us examine the topic of fear of failure in life through the lens of Sophia. Sophia recently graduated from college but has always been very successful. She was involved in numerous extracurricular activities and consistently performed well in school. She was determined to achieve her objectives and had a clear strategy for the future. However, she struggles with a fear of failure now that she has graduated and is beginning her job search.

Sophia is feeling anxious and overwhelmed because of her fear of failing. She worries that she won't be successful in her career or that she won't be able to get a job in her field. She is therefore experiencing resistance and feeling stuck.

Several things, including Sophia's lack of experience in the real world, her high expectations of herself, and her fear of disappointing others, are likely to blame for her fear of failure. She might also be feeling inadequate and comparing herself to other people.

Sophia must take several steps to get over her fear of failing. She must first acknowledge that failure is a normal part of life and that everyone at some point experiences it. Second, she must establish goals that are attainable and divide them into manageable steps. She will feel less overwhelmed and more in control because of this. Thirdly, rather than focusing solely on the outcome, she must concentrate on the learning and development process. Finally, she must seek assistance from friends, family, or, if necessary, a professional.

By taking these measures, Sophia may overcome her fear of failure and move on in her work and life with more confidence and resiliency.

A common experience that can prevent people from pursuing their goals and realizing their full potential is fear of failure. It can be brought on by several things, including previous failures, unrealistic expectations of oneself or others, and a lack of self-assurance.

Thankfully, there are several techniques for overcoming failure phobia. Such examples include viewing failure as a chance to learn and grow, practicing self-compassion and self-care, getting assistance from friends or a therapist, setting realistic objectives, and breaking things down into smaller pieces.

Recognizing that we all make mistakes from time to time and that failure is a normal part of learning is essential. We can increase our resilience, perseverance, and sense of worth by learning to conquer our fear of failure.

www.ingramcontent.com/pod-product-compliance
Lightning Source LLC
Chambersburg PA
CBHW062138160726
48282CB00027B/865
* 9 7 8 9 3 5 8 1 2 8 2 9 1 *